REUSABLE
DATA STRUCTURES
FOR C

Roger Sessions

Prime Computer Incorporated
Framingham, MA.

PRENTICE HALL, Englewood Cliffs, New Jersey 07632

Library of Congress Cataloging-in-Publication Data

SESSIONS, ROGER.
    Reusable data structure for C / Roger Sessions.
      p. cm.—(Prentice-Hall software series)

    Includes index.
ISBN 0-13-779034-1
    1. C (Computer program language) 2. Data structures (Computer
science) I. Title. II. Series.
QA76.73.C15S45 1989
005.13'3—dc19
                                     88-38498
                                        CIP

Editorial/production supervision and
   interior design: BARBARA MARTTINE
Cover design: DAN SANTORA
Cover photo: SAM CHEHAB
Manufacturing buyer: MARY ANN GLORIANDE

Prentice Hall Software Series
Brian Kernighan, Advisor

©1989 by Prentice-Hall, Inc.
A Division of Simon & Schuster
Englewood Cliffs, New Jersey 07632

Printed in the United States of America

10 9 8 7 6 5 4 3 2 1

ISBN   0-13-779034-1

Prentice-Hall International (UK) Limited, *London*
Prentice-Hall of Australia Pty. Limited, *Sydney*
Prentice-Hall Canada Inc., *Toronto*
Prentice-Hall Hispanoamericana, S,A., *Mexico*
Prentice-Hall of India Private Limited, *New Delhi*
Prentice-Hall of Japan, Inc., *Tokyo*
Simon & Schuster Asia Pte. Ltd., *Singapore*
Editora Prentice-Hall do Brasil, Ltda., *Rio de Janeiro*

Contents

Contents   **v**

Acknowledgments

Many close friends and acquaintances contributed to the nurture of this book. I found this experience humbling, as I realized how many people were involved with this effort in one way or another, and how dependent on their support I was.

Most of all, I am grateful to my wife, Alice Sessions, for her unending support, her long hours of editorial work, her constant encouragement, and her good humor throughout.

I also owe special thanks to Scott Gimpel, who helped me with the initial development of this book; to Karl Karlstrom and Ed Christiansen, for their early encouragement; to Ira Caplan and Lois Raney, for enthusiastically discussing many of the points of this book for hours on end; to Andy Koenig, P. J. Plauger, Brian Kernighan, Tsong-Shyan Wang and Mike Frame, for reviewing this manuscript; to Frank Calvillo, for his help using the printers; and to John Wait of Prentice-Hall, for his patience and encouragement. I am grateful to Prime Computer, Inc., for providing me with computer and other technical resources and for encouraging me in this effort. Many other colleagues at Prime Computer contributed to this work in small and not so small ways.

I would also like to thank these authors and publishers for their kind permission to reproduce excerpts from the following copyrighted material:

Data Structures and Algorithms by Niklaus Wirth in Scientific American, September 1984. Copyright © 1984 by Scientific American, Inc. All rights reserved.

On the Composition of Well-Structured Programs by Niklaus Wirth in ACM Computing Surveys, December 1974. Copyright © 1974 by Association for Computing Machinery, Inc. Reprinted with permission.

The Elements of Programming Style by Brian W. Kernighan and P. J. Plauger, Copyright © 1978 McGraw-Hill, Inc. Reprinted with permission.

Fall in Czechoslovakia by Jan Kuthan in Mushroom, The Journal, Fall, 1986. Copyright © 1986 by Mushroom. Reprinted with permission.

Some of the material in Chapter 3 was originally published in The Proceedings of CL Publications Inc.'s C Seminar/Workshop, San Francisco, 1986. Copyright © 1986 by Roger Sessions. Reprinted with permission.

CHAPTER 1 **Introduction**

Every C program has two primary functions: to control program flow and to organize and manipulate information. Most professionally written C programs have well organized program flow modules, particularly at the lowest levels. Functionality is compromised, however when data organization is poor. Data often tend to be disorganized, confused, and enmeshed with higher level program logic. Consolidating data manipulation responsibility into specialized but generalized modules greatly increases the overall reliability and reusability of the code. It also enhances data organization and flow.

How can a module have both specialized and generalized data manipulation responsibility? A module is specialized by virtue of its single-mindedness. The modules explored in this book have limited functionality. They manipulate linked lists, caches, queues, stacks, or binary trees. But they are generalized in that all application specificity has been stripped from them.

This book shows how these generalized modules can be used to solve a myriad of seemingly unrelated problems. For example, a linked list used to solve a personnel information management problem also serves as the basis for a dynamic memory manager; a cache developed to search text for overused words is also used to dramatically improve the performance of disk I/O; and, a queue used to solve a specialized text display problem becomes the foundation for a hospital emergency room controller.

These modules can also serve as building blocks for other, more complex structures. For instance, the cache can become a hash cache, the queue a priority queue. The linked list is a basic building block that can be used time and time again.

Good programming requires an understanding of the use, and implementation of data manipulation structures. The same structures reappear again and again. Like mushrooms, once you learn to recognize them, they seem to be everywhere. When these structures are well designed, the information flow through a program seems effortless, well oiled, reliable, and even aesthetically beautiful. When these structures are poorly designed, programs seem chaotic, uncontrolled, unmanageable, and untested. Niklaus Wirth discusses this issue in *Scientific American* (September 1984):

> Most large software systems rely on few ''deep'' algorithms; rather they are built up out of basic algorithms such as multiplication and searching, which appear in many variations and

1

combinations. The data structures, on the other hand, tend to be exceedingly complex. As a result the choice of the right data representation is often the key to successful programming, and it may have a greater influence on the program's performance than the details of the algorithm employed.

It is unlikely there will ever be a general theory for choosing data structures. The best that can be done is to understand the basic building blocks and the structures built up from them.

1.1. OVERVIEW

This book describes some techniques for organizing data manipulation code into one or more layers of code packages. The term *package* is used instead of *module*. Module usually refers to a collection of routines living in a single file. With packages, at least two files are involved; a generic definition of structure, which lives in a header file, and a code file containing the routines themselves. To eliminate confusion, the term *package* refers to a collection of code that, taken as a whole, is used to declare and manipulate a particular data structure, regardless of the number of files involved.

Reusable Data Structures for C shows how C can be used to effectively implement and organize common data structures. Familiarity with C is assumed. The data structures are all described in full, so it is not necessary to have studied data structures before using this material. In fact, this book can serve as an excellent introduction to the field, since many important data structures are covered in detail. The author has purposely chosen structures which, in his experience, are used most commonly. Nevertheless, the focus is on programming techniques rather than surveying data structures, and this book should not be seen as a comprehensive and advanced treatment of data structures.

Unlike most data structures books, this book focuses on the practical, rather than the theoretical. As such this book can also serve as useful adjunct material for a course on data structures, especially if C is one of the programming languages used.

Although Pascal and Ada are the languages usually associated with higher level data structures, we consider C uniquely adapted to implementing data structures in nonacademic environments. Much of this book discusses issues such as reusable modules and data structuring techniques which are specific to C.

This book demonstrates many advanced features of C, including dynamically allocated structures, memory management, and pointers to functions which show the language use to its fullest potential. These features tend to be slighted in other C books.

The coding techniques presented in this book can be used to develop highly reliable general purpose tools for managing information. This book especially emphasizes the need for developing reusable code, an important strength of C. In the examples such code is used extensively. We are, in effect, creating a metalanguage on top of C, one which is specialized for the description and management of information.

Although we reuse code wherever possible, this book does not suggest a bottom-up approach to programming. On the contrary, data design needs to be an integral part of overall systems design—planned at the highest level of system overview. This design philosophy is particularly important with large systems involving many programmers.

The purpose of *Reusable Data Structures for C* is to introduce reusable programming techniques for data manipulation. We stress straightforward implementations and use clear examples. Each chapter concludes with several programming examples designed to reinforce important concepts, introduce more advanced ideas, or present previously described topics in a new light. As these programs inevitably become larger and more complex, an awareness of data structures and an understanding of alternative implementations will become critical skills for the C programmer. These are the skills we introduce. Wherever possible, we build on previously described packages.

Chapter 2 discusses the theory of program correctness. It seems clear, almost axiomatic, that the techniques presented in this book result in more generalized code. This chapter presents evidence that these techniques also result in code that works better. In fact, we believe greatly improved code quality is justification enough for these techniques, even if the reader will never reuse a single line of code.

Chapter 3 introduces the practice of creating reusable data manipulation packages. This chapter looks at a particular programming problem—to scan text looking for overused words. The example demonstrates the decomposition of a problem into a series of subproblems, and specifically emphasizes the generalization and modularization of the data organization. Two packages are created, one for linked lists and one for caches. The characteristics of linked lists are discussed at length. A generic linked list package is developed in the form of a skeleton, which can be fleshed out with application specific information at compile time.

Chapters 4 and 5 show how application specific information and definitions can be moved from compile time to run time. Application specific information includes the sizes of items being stored, the number of items being stored, and the resolution of application specific data manipulation functions, such as item comparison functions. The techniques presented in these two chapters are essential to the remainder of this book. They will be used in subsequent chapters to produce highly flexible data manipulation packages with few limitations.

Many of the programming techniques used in this book will be criticized by some readers for performance reasons. They will claim the highly modular coding style results in unnecessary procedure calls, and therefore poor performance. Chapter 6 explores these concerns. The performance of the problem presented in Chapter 3 is discussed. The actual degradation due to packet design is analyzed, and shown to be insignificant. In most cases, performance is determined by the overall algorithm and the choice of data structures, not on the modularization of these structures. However, in those few cases where performance concerns are valid, we show how macro definitions can be created to improve performance with only minimal impact on modularity.

In Chapter 7, the highly flexible linked list package developed in Chapters 3, 4 and 5 is used in two more applications. Two objectives are inherent in this chapter. The first is to realize a further sense of what a linked list is, how it is used, and the behavior expected of it. The second is to reinforce reusablilty, showing how the package, without modification, can be used as the basis for two additional, unrelated programs.

Chapter 8 discusses the cache data structure created in Chapter 3, providing more detail, and modifying the original code to make a cache package that is fully functional and reusable. We look at the use of caches in speeding up input and output (I/O). This chapter also gives the first example of building reusable data manipulation packages from other packages.

Chapters 9 and 10 discuss and implement two more data manipulation packages: stacks and queues. Both use the updated linked list package of Chapters 4 and 5. The stack package solves problems in both memory allocation and database recovery. The queue package solves an interesting problem in text scanning, and is used as a building block for a more complex data structure, a priority queue.

Chapter 11 discusses recursive data structures, using a binary tree as an example. This chapter is needed for several reasons. First, many readers will be unfamiliar with recursive data structures, and even fewer will have considered modularizing such structures. Second, every data manipulation package used up to this point is based on the linked list package. The binary tree is an example of a fully reusable data manipulation package that does not use linked lists. Finally, because we build the binary tree from scratch, we have a second opportunity to see the techniques of Chapters 4 and 5 applied.

Chapter 12 discusses the common design features of the different data manipulation packages presented. The resulting roadmap can serve as a guideline for package design, which can be applied when designing any data manipulation package.

In Chapter 13, the author seeks to leave you with a limited set of rules, principles, and C programming techniques that will help you approach the problem of data organization with a new respect for reusability and modularity.

CHAPTER 2 **Program Correctness**

2.1. INTRODUCTION

The overall purpose of this book is to introduce methods for creating reusable data structures. We will see the advantages of reusability over and over again, as seemingly complex problems can be solved relatively quickly with code designed to manipulate generic data structures.

The procedures we will be presenting have limited functionality. For example, consider llnext(), a procedure from Chapter 5.

```
llnext()
{
   if (list->clp->next == NULL)
      return (0);
   else {
      list->clp = list->clp->next;
      return(1);
   }
}
```

As we will see later, this function updates the generic link list pointers to effectively move down the list. Because this code is absolutely generic, it deals with a very focused environment. It is influenced by one variable which has two significant states. It modifies one pointer and returns one of two possible values. It is essentially a very simple procedure and is typical of the functions we will be looking at.

This book presents a methodology for creating reusable data structures. This chapter presents a side benefit of following this methodology—the code you develop is more likely to work correctly. In addition, the code is written in a style that is amenable to an inspection process that *demonstrates* the correctness of the code. This chapter shows how this inspection process can be applied to the small, well defined functions typical of those in this book.

2.2. STRUCTURED PROGRAMMING

Most of us appreciate the principles of program modularization. We may describe these principles as *top-down programming, step-wise refinement*, or *structured programming*. These terms are essentially synonymous, all describing a basic approach to program organization and development. They describe a commitment to logical, unidirectional program flow, and a belief that the quality of a program is directly related to the care, skill, and determination of the author.

Some practitioners take a pragmatic approach to achieving program modularization, suggesting that specific programming rules be followed. Among the more familiar rules are these:

- Do not use GOTOs.
- Do not write functions which exceed a certain number of lines.
- Do not use global variables.

Many lines of unreadable, unmanageable, and unmaintainable code exist that adhere strictly to every one of these rules. We can also find examples of well organized, finely crafted code that technically violates all of these rules. Both novice and professional programmers can benefit by considering these rule guidelines, rather than ends in themselves. The experienced programmer understands not only the rules, but the motivation behind the rules, and can recognize the exceptional situations when these rules should not apply.

No formal checklist exists than can reliably tell us if a program is well structured, although it is most likely well structured if a competent reader can follow the logic without becoming bogged down in the details.

The best organized programs seem the simplest. They appear to solve a series of obvious problems, and invoke in the reader a reaction of "What's the big deal—I can do that". It is the disheveled and disorganized programs that seem superficially impressive, because we tend to attribute our lack of understanding to intellectual superiority on the part of the author. Our respect for such programs is misplaced. Far greater skill is needed to maintain control of the programming process and to methodically craft each function as a self-contained problem with an understandable solution.

Good programmers are always aware of the limited capacity of the human mind. Our ability to appreciate relationships deteriorates as the number of items involved increases. Consider this "structured" description of a forest:

- A forest is made up of trees and other plant life.
- Trees are made of leaves, branches, and trunks.

- Leaves are made up of a waterproof jacket, veins, and cells devoted to photosynthesis.
- The cells devoted to photosynthesis are made up primarily of structural molecules and molecules, that capture energy.
- The structural molecules of these cells are mostly carbohydrates.
- The molecules that capture energy are primarily chlorophyll, a molecule similar in structure to hemoglobin.

Compare this structured description to the following, which considers the same view from an ''un-structured'' perspective:

> A forest is made up of polypeptides, lipoproteins, complex carbohydrates, fatty acids and mono saccharide chains held together by glycosidic linkages, phosphoric acid esters, hydrated mycelles, deoxyribonucleic acid, structural polysaccharides, and of course, the omnipresent cellulases, all cooperating in a continuing exchange of exogenously combined nitrogen.

The structured forest description is intellectually manageable at all levels. The unstructured description leaves us floundering, without having any idea what we are talking about; we literally cannot see the forest for the trees.

The term *step-wise refinement* is used by Niklaus Wirth to describe a structured approach to programming. We can actually describe a formal algorithm for this stepwise refinement process of program development. By carefully following this recursive algorithm, even the most complex problems are solvable in due time. The algorithm for stepwise refinement looks like this

```
solve_problem(problem)
{
    if (problem = = trivial) write solution;
    else {
      breakdown_problem_into_N_subproblems;
      define_relationship_between_subproblems;
      for (each_subproblem)
          solve_problem(subproblem);
    }
}
```

Let us look at an example of this refinement methodology. Consider writing a program named scanner to perform text scans. This program will ask the user for the name of a text file and a search string. The program will then print the file line by line. Each line will be preceded by five characters indicating the presence (or absence) of the search string. Lines containing the search string will be preceded by ''-->'', others by blanks.

A typical scanner run looks like this

run scanner
    Text File: **meeting.860912**
Search String: **Amanita**
        Sunday's foray consisted of a pleasant walk
        through the Greenvale woods and surrounding
        meadows. Participants were surprised at the
        quantity and quality of Agaricus campestris
        collected and by the relative sparseness of
--> Amanitas. The one exception was the hardwoods
        near the Hodgkins estate, which abounded
--> in Amanita muscaria. It was truly unfortunate
        that this stately mushroom could be appreciated
        only for its beauty, and not its culinary qualities.

At the highest level, our problem is to produce scanner. Solving this problem with the refinement methodology gives these results

  1. solve_problem() is called with scanner().

  2. The problem is not trivial, so we break scanner() down into subproblems and define a new relationship, for example

```
solve_problem(scanner()) =
{
  get_user_input();
  open_text_file();
  scan_text_file();
  close_file();
}
```

  3. solve_problem is recursively called with each of the subproblems, starting with get_user_input().

  4. solve_problem(get_user_input()) is trivial. It writes out two prompts and stores the resulting string. solve-problem(open_text_file()) is also trivial.

  5. solve-problem(scan_text_file()) is not trivial. A new related series of subproblems is created.

```
solve_problem(scan_text_file =))
{
  while ((input_line = read_line =)) != DONE) {
    if (search_string_found())
      write_arrow();
    else
      write_blank();
    write_input_line();
  }
}
```

6. Having   defined   this   relationship   for   `scan_text_file()`, `solve_problem()`   is   recursively   called   with   `read_line()`, `search_string_found()`,   `write_arrow()`,   `write_blank()`,   and `write_input_line()`. Each of these subproblems is trivial, so we have finished `solve_problem()` of `scan_text_file()`.

7. We return to `solve_problem()`, having just completed the solution to `scan_text_file()`. We can `solve_problem()` once more with `close_file()`, which is trivial, and we are finished.

It should be clear that after following this algorithm, we end up with a subproblem hierarchy, which is readily interpretable as the following function invocation hierarchy:

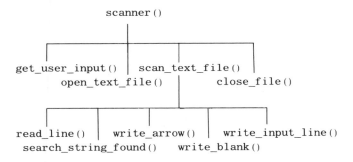

In the December 1974 issue of ACM Computing Surveys, Niklaus Wirth describes both the ideal and reality of this process very well:

> In passing, I should like to stress that we should not be led to infer that actual program conception proceeds in such a well organized, straightforward "top-down" manner. Later refinement steps may often show that earlier decisions are inappropriate and must be reconsidered. But this neat, nested factorization of a program serves admirably well to keep the individual building blocks intellectually manageable, to explain the program to an audience and to oneself, to raise the level of confidence in the program, and to conduct informal, and even formal proofs of correctness.

2.3. PROVABILITY

Although many of us feel intuitively that modularization results in more reliable programs, it is interesting to speculate on Wirth's statement that we can "conduct informal, and even formal proofs of correctness." How is our ability to prove the correctness of a program or function dependent on its organization? The remainder of this chapter describes one informal approach to this proof process.

We can informally prove a function (or program) is correct if we can show two propositions about it are true.

Proposition 1   The function calls only "correct" functions. In other words, external expectations are fulfilled.

Proposition 2   If this function invokes only "correct" functions, this function will work correctly. In other words, the internal logic is correct.

The following graph represents an invocation sequence for a typical program and serves as an example for the discussion that follows.

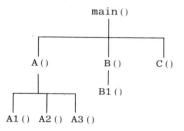

In describing the proof process for a program, we will use these definitions:

> *root function:* The single function at the highest level of invocation: main() in the example.
>
> *terminal function:* A function that does not invoke any other function: for example, A1(), A2(), A3(), B1(), and C().
>
> *near terminal function:* A function that invokes only terminal function(s): A() and B().
>
> *non-terminal function:* A function that invokes any function(s). Root functions and near terminal functions are both non-terminal.

Assume the program whose function hierarchy is shown in the example was developed using the refinement algorithm. Proposition 1 tells us that the correctness of the root function is dependent on its invoked functions. In this case then, the correctness of A(), B(), and C() must be established before we can show that main() works. To show that A() works, we need to show that A1(), A2(), and A3() all work. Let us start with a terminal function, say A1().

The inspection process is simplified for terminal functions. Proposition 1 does not apply to terminal functions, because, by definition, they do not invoke other functions. Therefore we can limit our examination to Proposition 2. The validity of Proposition 2 for a given terminal function can be determined through inspection. If the function was developed according to the rules of the refinement algorithm, it should be a so-called trivial function, or one that can be fully inspected in all of its states.

The *state* of a function is its particular combination of input variables. For example, the function llnext(), shown earlier, has two significant states: list->clp->next is equal to NULL, and list->clp->next is not equal to NULL.

Once we know how to conduct this proof by inspection, we can show the correctness of any terminal function. And, once we have inspected all terminal functions, we have also demonstrated Proposition 1 (that all invoked functions work correctly) for all near terminal functions, say A().

The refinement algorithm tells us that because A() is non-terminal, it must be a function which describes the relationship between a series of subproblems. If this relationship is described clearly and carefully, we can informally prove Proposition 2, once again by inspection.

We have now shown how to prove the correctness of both terminal and near terminal functions. Near terminal functions are provable because we know how to prove the correctness of their subfunctions, terminal functions. By extension, we can prove the correctness of any non-terminal function, including the root.

The following steps summarize the inspection process:

1. Enumerate all possible states for the function. This process will be examined in more detail in the next session.

2. For each state, determine if the function works correctly.
a. If a state is found for which the function is hopelessly complex, the inspection is finished; the function is un-inspectable.
b. If a state is found for which the function works incorrectly, the inspection is finished; the function doesn't work.

3. For each invoked function, go through the process described in Step 2.
a. If a function is found for which condition 2a is true, then this function must be considered un-inspectable until the offending function can be re-written in fully inspectable form.
b. If a function is found for which condition 2b is true, then this function must be considered not to work correctly.

4. If all states for a function pass the inspection, and all invoked functions recursively pass the inspection algorithm, then this function has been fully inspected, and its correctness demonstrated.

2.4. FUNCTION STATES

The number of possible states of a function depends on the number of variables accessed by the function, and the number of values each variable can contain. Although most variables can be assigned a large range of values, we can usually limit our inspection to only significant values, such as those at the beginning and end of a loop. A function with M variables, each with N possible significant values, has N^M significant states. Each of these states must be examined before Proposition 2 can be accepted.

For example, a function with three variables, each of which can take the value 0 or 1, has these eight possible states:

Var1	Var2	Var3
0	0	0
0	0	1
0	1	0
0	1	1
1	0	0
1	0	1
1	1	0
1	1	1

We can now consider the ramifications of program design on program inspectability. Consider a hypothetical programming problem that requires ten variables, each taking four significant values. If we write a function with these ten variables, we must consider 4^{10}, or 1,048,576, significant states.

Suppose this same problem could be solved by writing a root function that invokes ten terminal functions, each containing one of these same variables. With this solution, we would have to inspect eleven functions instead of one. The root function would have no variables, and therefore only one state. The terminal functions would each have one variable, taking four significant values. Each terminal function would have 4^1, or 4 states. Because there are ten of these functions, we would have to examine $10(4^1)$, or 40 total states plus 1 for the root function.

Either approach uses the same number of variables with the same number of significant values. In the first case, we must examine over 1,000,000 states. In the second case, we must examine 41 states. The organization of variables into well defined functions transforms complex functions into functions that are demonstrably correct. A nice side effect of the programming style presented in this book is that variables are naturally organized, and the number of function states naturally small.

The provability of functions is constrained by the organization of the variables, and by extension, the organization of the data. Functions written in C have two sources for variables:

- Local variables, those declared within the function.
- Global variables, those declared in the header section of the module containing the function.

It should be clear that global variables severely strain function inspectability, because each must be considered for every function in the module. Global variables should be used only when necessary. In addition, indiscriminate use of local variables can quickly have the same effect.

We are left with this important result—by proper modularization and careful sequestering of data, we can create programs that are inspectable, and perhaps even provably correct. Meticulous modularity is the key, because it limits the interactions between variables. The functions in this book are as modular as any you are likely to encounter. Their purposes are very narrow. They manipulate only the generic parts of standard data structures.

2.5. THE INSPECTION PROCESS

This section looks at an example of how a typical function might be inspected. We will use the function `scan_text_file()`, created as part of the solution to `scanner` shown previously in this chapter.

The specifications for `scan_text_file()` are straightforward. The routine should loop through input lines. If a given line contains the search string, that line should be preceded by a printed arrow. Otherwise it should be preceded by blanks. The routine looked like this

```
scan_text_file()
{
  while ((input_line = read_line()) != Done) {
    if (search_string_found())
      write_arrow();
    else
      write_blank();
    write_input_line();
  }
}
```

There are two variables in this function: `input_line` and `search_string_found()`. One of these "variables" is, in fact, a function. For the purpose of counting states however, the values returned by the function will be treated like variables. The variable states are summarized in the following table:

Input_Line	Search_String_Found()
DONE	TRUE
!DONE	TRUE
DONE	FALSE
!DONE	FALSE

The table shows four variable states, which is what we would predict given two variables, each with two states. The table can be expanded to show what `scan_text_file()` does in each probable case:

Case #	Input_Line	Search_String_Found()	Arrows Printed?	Input Printed?	Continue Loop?
1	DONE	TRUE	no	no	no
2	!DONE	TRUE	yes	yes	yes
3	DONE	FALSE	no	no	no
4	!DONE	FALSE	no	yes	yes

Each of these function states needs validation. When `input_line` contains DONE, neither arrows nor input are printed and the loop terminates, regardless of what search_string_found() does. Actually search_string_found() is never called. There-fore, Cases 1 and 3 are the same and both are valid.

There are two cases where input_line is set to !DONE. In both cases the loop contin-ues. For Case 2, search_string_found() returns TRUE and both arrows and input are printed. This result in accordance with the specifications, so Case 2 is valid. For Case 4, search_string_found() returns FALSE. The arrows are not printed, but the input is. Again this is according to specification and Case 4 is valid.

You can formally inspect code many ways. This example demonstrates one method. Most importantly, every significant function state needs to be examined and shown to fulfill the requirements of the algorithm.

2.6. REUSABILITY

Although data modularization is of premier importance for correctness inspections, an-other concept, reusability, can also be a significant factor in writing inspectable functions. Reusability is, of course, a major topic of this book. This section focuses on the role of reusability in correctness inspections. If, in the past, we created functions which were proven correct, and we can now reuse those functions, then the correctness proof is simplified further. Suppose we have the following invocation sequence:

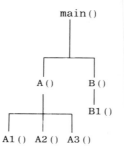

If A1(), A2(), A3() and B1() are existing modules that were already proven to be correct, then we can show main() invokes correct functions by inspecting only two of the six functions it calls. Such reusable functions are particularly attractive because not only have they been proven correct, but they have also withstood the test of time. And for all our faith in correctness inspections, the best proof of all is still in the pudding.

For example, when writing a program to conduct key-word analysis on text files, key-words can be implemented as sets which, in turn, can be designed from linked lists. A reusable collection of proven linked list manipulating functions can be the foundation of our set manipulation module which, if designed reusably, can find life in future applica-tions.

We can prove the correctness of such a program by first showing that the linked list module works. Next, we show that the set module works, and finally, that the key-word searching algorithm works. Each of these testing demonstrations is a small, manageable task that assumes lower level modules function properly.

2.7. SUMMARY

There are two important advantages of writing provably correct programs—modularity, and reusability. Actually, it is not the author's intent to insist on applying a rigorous correctness inspection to every piece of code. However, there is little doubt that the application of these principles results in code of superior quality, and that the quality of the code is directly related to the inspectability of the code. This is true even when the inspection process is not rigorously followed. The remainder of this book will be devoted to showing how we can use the C programming language to create reusable, self-contained (and thus provably correct) data manipulation packages, and how these packages can form the basis of reliable, maintainable programs.

2.8. EXERCISES

1. We said that the number of significant statements for a program with M variables, each of which can contain N significant values, is N^M. We simplified the equation by assuming that each variable contained the same number of significant values. Assume instead that the program contains M variables. The first can contain N_1 significant values, the second N_2, and so on. What is the true number of significant states for such a program?

2. Suppose a program is composed of five functions, each using three variables, which have two significant states. How many states must be considered for a full inspection? Suppose three of the functions are re-treads, and were already inspected. Now how many states need to be considered?

CHAPTER 3 **Introduction to Package Programming**

3.1. REVIEW

In the last chapter we discussed programming techniques which lend themselves to writing verifiable code. Two concepts were central in the chapter—modularity and reusability. Modularity is perhaps the most critical because it results in the development of functions that have the following two characteristics:

1. Because each function accesses very few variables, a limited number of states needs to be examined during the inspection process.

2. The functions tend to be individually simple, even trivial, resulting in fully inspectable variable states.

3.2. USING DATA CONCEPTS

This chapter looks at how these concepts can be applied to real problems. Consider writing a program to scan text files looking for overused words. Say a word is overused if it appears more than once within any given stretch of 25 unique words. A typical input text file might look like the following:

> User Friendly Software, Inc. announces the most completely user friendly, powerful software available. A child can easily and simply create powerful applications that can easily handle any need completely, and still be completely user friendly and powerful. To receive this powerful software, simply mail this coupon.

Some of the overused words this program should return from this text file are:
    user, friendly, software, powerful, can, easily, completely, simply

A structured pseudocode solution to this problem is

```
while ((word = getword(text_file)) != DONE) {
  if (word_is_overused)
    print_word(word);
  note_word_was_just_used;
}
```

Most of us can write a routine `getword()` to read a text file and return the next word as a null terminated string pointer. It is less clear how to tell if a `word_is_overused`, and what it means to `note_word_was_just_used`.

Before we plunge into solving this problem, we should stop to think carefully about the kind of tools that could be useful. We will purposely defer considering the practicality of such tools. Practicality is a separate issue. Two cardinal rules should guide our approach:

1. Think like a human being rather than a computer. Don't say, "If I were a computer, what would I use to help solve this problem?" Say instead, "As a human being, how would I approach this problem?"

2. Think about the tools you want to build rather than the tools you know how to build. Forget about implementation. You may indeed find that you have specified the impossible, but more likely, when the separate problem of implementation comes up, you will discover unknown reserves of creativity within yourself.

The hardest part of solving this problem is trying to remember the last 25 unique words in the text. Each new word needs to be checked against the last 25 unique words, and be remembered for future reference. We only need to store 25 words at any given time. For each new word on the list, an old word can be forgotten. That word would be the one which has not been used for the longest time, the 26th unique word.

What kind of tools would help? It seems we need some kind of storage structure for words, a Word Box, and in particular, a Word Box with these specifications:

- Words can be inserted into the box.
- The box can hold a maximum of 25 words.
- The box can tell us when a word is inside.
- If we try to insert more words than the box can hold, the box makes room by dumping the least recently referenced words. By "referenced," we mean either inserted or inquired about.

The following diagram shows how the contents of the box change as words are referenced. The right side of the diagram shows the words currently in the box in order of future discard. For example, in the series

```
horse cat dog
```

the next word available for discard is *dog*. As a word is added to the left, it becomes the least available for discard, and all other words move one position closer to discard. When a word is eventually discarded, the last in the series falls off.

Figure 3-1: Word Box Trace for A 3 Word Box

Action	Box Contents
add(dog)	dog
add(cat)	cat dog
add(horse)	horse cat dog
me: Is **cat** there? box: yes	cat horse dog
add(pig)	pig cat horse
me: Is **dog** there? box: no	pig cat horse
add(human) add(mouse)	human pig cat mouse human pig
me: Is **pig** there? box: yes	pig mouse human
add(fish)	fish pig mouse
me: Is **human** there? box: no	fish pig mouse

   With such a Word Box our problem is easily solved. A word_is_overused if it is in the box. To note_word_was_just_used the word is added to the box. The pseudocode for this problem, making use of this hypothetical Word Box, looks like the following:

```
while ((word = getword(text_file)) != DONE) {
  if (word_is_overused)
     print_word(word);
  note_word_was_just_used();
}

note_word_was_just_used()
{
  see_if_word_is_in_box();
  if (not)
     add_word_to_box();
}

see_if_word_is_overused()
{
  see_if_word_is_in_box();
}
```

3.3. THE CACHE

Aficionados of data concepts will recognize the Word Box as a variation on a cache. The word *cache* is derived from the French word *cacher*, meaning to conceal. In Computer Science, cache has come to describe a storage structure for holding a small number of items, usually some subset of a larger set. In this specific case the larger set is the set of all words in the advertisement and the subset is the collection of the 25 most recently used words.

Every item in a cache has a unique key. For the Word Box cache the key is the word itself. Items can be queried and retrieved by key. Each item in a cache has a unique availability for discard, which may vary with time. When items are displaced, the most "discardable" item is the one displaced. Different algorithms are used to determine discardability. A common algorithm, and the one used in this case, considers discardability to be related to time of reference. The longer an item has been in the cache without being referenced, the more discardable it is. This algorithm is often referred to as LRU, for Least Recently Used.

Caches are frequently used to speed up I/O processing, but they obviously have other applications as well. Chapter 8 is devoted completely to this interesting data structure.

Once we recognize the Word Box as a cache, we are several steps ahead of the game. First, we know what behavior to expect from our box. Second, we probably have some thoughts on how the implementation might proceed. Finally, by generalizing the development of the cache, we can create code which can be recycled the next time we stumble across a cache application.

Conceptually, a cache can be implemented as a string of items with the position within the string indicating the discard value. Items are added to the front of the string and discarded from the end. Notice how the following string changes as we work with the cache:

```
add_item(dog);          dog
add_item(cat);          cat——dog
add_item(horse);        horse—cat——dog
check_id(cat);          cat——horse—dog
add_item(pig);          pig——cat——horse
check_id(dog);          pig——cat——horse
```

Some common cache operators are:

`add_item()`	Adds a new item to the cache.
`check_id()`	Checks the cache. Returns TRUE if the ID is already in the cache, FALSE otherwise.
`get_item()`	Returns the item matching the requested ID.

The rest of this chapter demonstrates the Word Box implemented as a cache, and the cache implemented as a two-way linked list. Other valid implementations exist, however the implementation details are less important than the data organization. The Word Box user does not care how the box is implemented as long as the Word Box itself is understandable and dependable.

The previous chapter showed how reusable packages contributed to the ease of verifying code. The concept of generalization goes hand in hand with reusability. Caches for example are general purpose data structures, implementable as linked lists. Linked lists, in turn, can also be implemented as general purpose data structures.

Ideally a cache module should be both self contained (modular) and non-specific (generic). The module should perform only those data manipulations common to all caches, and be limited therefore in scope. The programming logic should be straightforward and require few variables—two conditions which have been shown to be important for code verifiability. When a packet is generic, it is also reusable, meaning today's efforts can be depreciated against future projects.

Any data structure, such as a cache, has a set of primitive operators usually implemented as function calls. We have already identified three standard cache primitives: add_item(), check_id(), and get_item(). The Word Box example requires only the first two.

When implementing a cache as a linked list, placement on the list indicates relative time of reference. The item at the head of the list is the item most recently referenced. The item at the tail is the item least recently referenced.

The procedure co_check() is easily implemented. It searches the list returning TRUE if it finds an item with the requested key, or FALSE if it hits the end of the list. Although the procedure ca_add() is more complicated because it acts differently in each of four cases, each of the cases is straightforward. The four cases ca_add() needs to contend with are

List empty	Item present	List full	Action
T	F	F	Create new list with item.
F	T	T/F	Promote link containing item to head.
F	F	T	Discard tail, add item to head.
F	F	F	Add item to head.

3.4. THE BOTTOM SOFTWARE LAYER: LINKED LISTS

We have now defined the behavior of caches and discussed an implementation based on linked lists. The same arguments that favor generic cache packages also support generic linked list packages. Perhaps these arguments are even stronger because the linked list is truly ubiquitous.

The concept of a two-way linked list is analogous in many ways to a train. A link in the list is like a car on the train. Finding an item in a two-way linked list is like finding an item on a train. Imagine for example that a passenger is trying to locate a friend on a train. The passenger has three choices at all times. The passenger can look in the current car. The passenger can move to the next car and look. Or, the passenger can move back to the previous car and look. If the passenger decides to move to a new car, the same three choices must be faced again. The passenger can never skip a car, and can never reach a car other than by moving through the train. A program's view of a linked list is similar to the passenger's view of the train.

The following table shows a reasonable collection of linked list primitives, each of which will be implemented as a function in the linked list module. Later we will use these primitives to develop a cache package.

`llnext()`	Move to the next link.
`llprevious()`	Move to the previous link.
`llretrieve()`	Retrieve the item in the current link.
`lladd()`	Create a new link with this item immediately after the current link.
`lldelete()`	Delete the current link. Join the previous and next links together.
`llhead()`	Move to the first link in the list. (Notice the train analogy starts to break down here.)
`lltail()`	Move to the last link in the list.
`ll_length()`	Return the number of links in the list.

In its most basic form, a link in a list consists of a block of memory subdivided into at least three sections. One section contains the address of the next link in the list, that is, the address of another similar block of memory. A second section contains the address of the previous link. The remaining section(s) contains application specific memory. In the case of the Word Box, this application specific area is used to store text strings (words). The first two areas are generic for any linked list application, and it is these areas for which the linked list package is responsible. The skeleton of a C module used to implement a generic linked list package looks like this

```
/* Linked List Module */
#include "lldef.h"
#include "stdio.h"

struct linktype {
  struct linktype *next;
  struct linktype *previous;
  struct itemtype item;
};

static struct linktype *clp = NULL;   /* Current Link Pointer    */
static struct linktype *head = NULL;  /* First link              */
static struct linktype *tail = NULL;  /* Last link               */

static int listlength = 0;            /* Number of links in list. */

/* Procedure definitions start here. */
...
/* End of procedure definitions. */
```

Four global variables are available to any of the functions defined in this module. Only one of these, clp, is essential. clp stands for the current link pointer. This variable contains the address of the block of memory considered the current link. next and previous operators alter the contents of clp, resetting it to the address of the next or previous link, respectively. Although we are calling clp a "global" variable, it is declared static, and is therefore protected from routines living outside of this module. Notice how the next() and previous() primitives affect the clp:

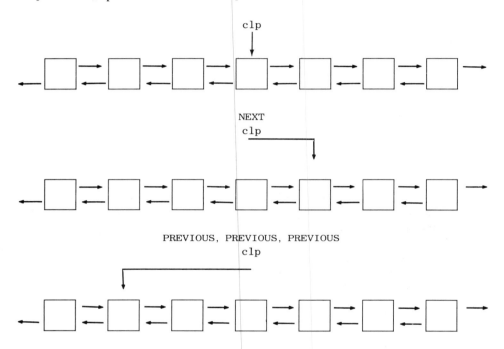

Other global variables, head, tail, and listlength are included for convenience only. Any of the linked list functions could be implemented using only clp, although many of them would take substantially longer to execute. The purposes of these auxiliary global variables are as follows:

head	Contains the address of the first link in the list.
tail	Contains the address of the last link in the list.
listlength	Contains the number of links currently in the list.

Previously we provided a list of linked list primitives. The next table shows how each of these primitives can be implemented and how they affect the various global variables:

llhead()	Set the current link pointer (clp) to the head of the list (head).

lltail()	Set clp to tail.
llnext()	Set clp to the next link, returning FALSE if clp is at the tail.
llprevious()	Set clp to the previous link, returning FALSE if clp is at the head.
llretrieve()	Retrieve the item at the clp.
lladd()	Add a new link containing this item immediately following the clp.
lldelete()	Delete the link at the clp.
ll_length()	Return listlength.

The linked list module skeleton contains this structure definition:

```
struct linktype {
  struct linktype *next;
  struct linktype *previous;
  struct itemtype item;
};
```

which is the basic description for a block of memory making a link. This definition does not allocate memory, it just defines how some block of memory will be interpreted later. The definition example tells us that this memory block will contain three structures: two variables, each containing the addresses of other similar memory blocks, and an embedded structure, an item, of type itemtype.

The type itemtype is defined in a separate file, lldef.h, which contains the information making the linked list application specific. For example, if we were creating word caches, lldef.h might look like the following:

```
/* File: lldef.h - Modified for word Caches*/

#define WORDLEN 30
struct itemtype {
  char string [WORDLEN];
};
```

On the other hand, for disk block caches such as those used to speed up disk I/O, lldef.h might appear as

```
/* File: lldef.h - Modified for Disk Block Caches*/

#define BLOCKLEN 256
struct itemtype {
  int fileid;
  int byte_offset;
  char block[BLOCKLEN];
};
```

The reason itemtype is defined as a structure, even in this simple case, is so that procedures such as llretrieve() can be set up as such

```
llretrieve(item)
struct itemtype *item;
{
. . .
}
```

This construction guarantees that llretrieve() and similar functions will never need modification, regardless of the complexity (or simplicity) of the information being stored in the linked list. In fact, the only changes needed to manipulate a linked list with a completely different itemtype are to modify the lldef.h file and recompile the module.

We will now examine each of the linked list operator functions. Assume each is in the same linked list module previously defined and can therefore access the global variables clp, head, tail, and listlength. As we proceed, we will informally inspect each function, following the guidelines of Chapter 2.

The first function, moveitem, is actually a macro definition, used internally within the module. It is a more manageable form of the standard library function movmem() and is designed to copy one item to another. It is essentially an arithmetic assignment function for itemtypes. This macro copies items, not links. Items are one of the components of links.

```
#define moveitem(A,B) movmem(A, B, sizeof(struct itemtype))
/* moveitem(from, to) */
```

Inspecting moveitem() is straightforward. No global variables are used, and about all we can do is convince ourselves that the correct arguments have been passed into sizeof(), and perhaps try a test case to verify that A and B are in the correct order.

Next is our runtime link space allocator. It is as easy to understand as moveitem(), and in fact, could have also been written as a macro definition. This function is declared static, because it is called only within this module. As for inspection, again, no global variables are used, and the inspection boils down to verifying the malloc() call and the type casting have both been done correctly.

```
static struct linktype *llcrlink() /* Allocate space for a link */
{
  return ((struct linktype *)
        malloc(sizeof(struct linktype)));
}
```

The next function, llinit(), is called when a program needs to initialize a linked list with an item.

```
llinit(newitem)     /* Initialize the linked list with an item */
struct itemtype *newitem;
{
  struct linktype *llcrlink();

  head = tail = clp = llcrlink();       /* There is only one link */
  clp->next = clp->previous = NULL;     /* No next or previous links */
  moveitem(newitem, &(clp->item));      /* Put this item into link */
  listlength  = 1;                      /* Initialize listlength */
}
```

This function is non-terminal. It calls two other functions, `llcrlink()` and `moveitem()`, both of which we have already inspected. We can accept Proposition 1 that says a function calls only correct functions. Our next step then is to consider the second proposition.

The global variables are unconditionally reset, so previous values do not matter. Following the terminology of Chapter 2, all variable states for this function are equivalent. Choose any one of them and consider it to be the significant state we will inspect. The algorithm is simple, even trivial, and we should be able to prove that if the functions called work correctly, this function will also work correctly. This statement agrees exactly with Proposition 2, thus we can consider the inspection complete.

The next two functions, `llhead` and `lltail` set link currency, `clp`, to either the head or tail of the list. They are basically trivial, depending only on `head` and `tail` having correct values.

```
llhead()
{
  clp = head;
}
lltail()
{
  clp = tail;
}
```

Next, we have a slightly interesting function, `llnext()`, which moves `clp` to the next link.

```
llnext() /* Move the CLP down the list */
{
  if (clp->next == NULL)
    return (0);             /* Return FALSE if at end of list */
  else {
    clp = clp->next;
    return (1);             /* Return TRUE if not at end */
  }
}
```

Though no other functions are called (and therefore Proposition 1 is accepted) we can enumerate several possible significant values for clp:

1. clp is pointing at the first link. clp->next will contain the address of another link, the link to which clp will be reset.

2. clp is pointing at the last link. clp->next will contain NULL, we cannot move clp, we will return FALSE.

3. clp is pointing at one of the central link(s). This condition is the same as the first state.

The function llprevious() is the mirror image of llnext().

```
llprevious()      /* Set the CLP to the previous link */
{
   if (clp->previous == NULL)
      return (0);           /* Return FALSE if at start of list */
   else {
      clp = clp->previous; /* Return TRUE otherwise */
      return (1);
   }
}
```

The next function, llretrieve(), copies the item in the current link (i.e., the link pointed to by clp) into a memory location provided by the caller. The only significant state occurs when clp points at a valid link.

```
llretrieve(newitem) /* Retrieve the item for the CLP link */
struct itemtype *newitem;
{
   moveitem(&(clp->item), newitem);
}
```

The function lladd() allocates space for a new link, copies newitem into the link, and inserts the link directly after the clp. All called functions have been inspected thus far. Two cases are significant: either the clp is pointing at the last link, or it is not. In the first case, tail should be updated to point to the new link; in the second case, it should be left alone, but the link following clp should have its previous pointer set to the new link. If you are not convinced that the pointers next and previous are set properly in both cases, write a small test program to verify this fact.

```
lladd(newitem)
struct itemtype *newitem;   /* Item to place in link. */
{
   struct linktype *newlink;
   struct linktype *llcrlink();
```

```
/* Create new link.
------------------  */
   new link = llcrlink();
   moveitem(newitem, &(newlink->item));
   listlength++;

/* Reset pointers.
-----------------  */
   newlink->next = clp->next;
   newlink->previous = clp;
   if (tail == clp)
      tail = newlink;
   else
      clp->next->previous = newlink;
   clp->next = newlink;
   clp = newlink;              /* Point CLP to new link */
}
```

Another function, `lladdhead()`, is similar to `lladd()`, but simpler to comprehend because only one significant variable case (i.e., head is valid) exists.

```
/* Add a new link to the head of the list */
lladdhead(newitem)
struct itemtype *newitem; /* Item to add */
{
   struct linktype *newlink;
   struct linktype *llcrlink();

/* If empty, initialize list.
   ------------------------  */
   if (ll_length() == 0) {
      llinit(newitem);
      return;
   }
/* Create new link.
   ----------------  */
   newlink = llcrlink();
   moveitem(newitem, &(newlink->item));
   listlength++;

/* Reset pointers.
   ----------------  */
   newlink->previous = NULL;
   newlink->next = head;
   head->previous = newlink;
   clp = head = newlink;
}
```

The function `ll_length()` is trivial. Its only purpose is to allow outside programs read only access to the global variable `listlength`.

```
ll_length() /* Return the number of links in list */
{
   'return (listlength);
}
```

The function `lldelete()` is the most complicated function in the module. It deletes and frees the `clp`, and then resets the `clp` to the head of the list. This function has four significant states:

1. `clp` can be pointing to the head of a list.

2. `clp` can be pointing to the tail of a list.

3. `clp` can be pointing to an inner link.

4. All of the above, i.e., `clp` can be pointing to the only link in a list.

```
lldelete()
{
   struct linktype *before, *after, *delete; /* For clarity */

/* Delete only link.
   ----------------   */
   delete = clp;
   if (head == clp && tail == clp) {
      head = tail = NULL;
   }
/* Is this the head?
   ---------------- */
   else if (head == clp) {
      clp = head = head->next;
      head->previous = NULL
   }
/* Is this the tail?
   ---------------- */
   else if (tail == clp) {
      clp = tail = tail->previous;
      tail->next = NULL;
   }
/* Otherwise, it must be inside the list.
   ------------------------------------- */
   else {
      before = clp->previous;
      clp = after = clp->next;
      before->next = after;
      after->previous = before;
   }
```

```
/* Delete CLP.
   ----------- */
   free(delete);
   listlength--;
}
```

lldelete() was written specifically to expedite the proof process, with each of the four possible cases carefully laid out. It could have been condensed at the expense of clarity and inspectability, but was not.

3.5. THE NEXT LAYER: THE CACHE PACKAGE

Our newly completed linked list package can now form the basis for a cache. Little additional work is needed because we have already taken care of most of the dirty details.

The start of the cache module looks like

```
/* Cache Module */
#include <lldef.h>
static int cachesize = 0; /* Number of elements allowed in cache */
casetsize(size) /* The outside world's access path to cachesize */
int size;
{
   cachesize = size;
}
```

These first lines form the header for the module. We are including the lldef.h file that contains the application specific information for the linked list, and also for the cache. The global variable cachesize will contain the size of the cache, and the function casetsize() is the mechanism provided for setting this variable. In our Word Box example, a call to casetsize() would pass in a value of 25.

The function ca_add() assumes that an item is not in the cache. This function has three variable states.

1. The cache (i.e., linked list) is empty, and is therefore initialized with the item.

2. The cache is full and an item must be discarded. As already described, the tail item is always discarded.

3. The cache is neither empty nor full, in which case we add this item to the head of the list.

We can prove that the function is valid for each of these cases, either by inspection or testing.

testing.

```
ca_add(newitem)
struct itemtype *newitem;
{
/* Add item to list.
   ---------------- */
   if (ll_length() == 0)
      llinit(newitem);
   else
      lladdhead(newitem);

/* Delete an old item if cache is overloaded.
   ---------------------------------------- */
   if (ll_length() > cachesize) {
      lltail();
      lldelete();
   }
}
```

The next function, ca_check(), searches the cache for a particular item, returning a value of true or false depending on the search results. If the item is found, it becomes the most recently referenced item and is promoted to the head of the list.

```
ca_check(lookfor)  /* See if item is in cache */
                   /* Return TRUE or FALSE
struct itemtype *lookfor;
{
   struct itemtype lookat;
   cmpitem();

   llhead();
   for (;;) {
      llretrieve (&lookat);
      if (cmpitem(lookfor, &lookat)) {
        lldelete()
        lladdhead(&lookat);
        return (1);
      }
      if (!llnext())
        return (0);
   }
}
```

One more function, cmpitem(), needs to be added to the cache module. It can either be placed in a separate module or in the top level word checking code.

```
cmpitem(item1, item2) /* Compare two items */
struct itemtype *item1, *item2;
{
    return(!strcmp(item1->string, item2->string));
}
```

The function cmpitem() actually compares two items. It is the logical equality operator for itemtypes. It should not be part of the cache package, even though called by ca_check(), because it is application specific. In this specific example two items are the same if their respective strings are equivalent.

Although the availability of the linked list package has saved considerable effort in developing the cache package the linked list package does have some unsatisfying characteristics. For one, when we think of a reusable package we usually think of using a single object file for many different programs. In this implementation, multiple object files must be maintained, each reflecting a different lldef.h file. However the cost is minor compared to our gains. We can actually improve on our methods even further, and this improvement will comprise the subject matter of the next two chapters.

3.6. EXERCISES

1. Consider the function cmpitem(). Instead of using strcmp(), why not use the standard library function memcmp(), which is presumably more efficient, to check sizeof(struct itemtype) number of bytes for equality?

2. Modify cmpitem() so that two items match if they match letter by letter, regardless of case. For example, "Hello" should match "HELLO".

3. The function ca_add() adds an item differently depending on whether it is initializing a new cache or adding an item to an existing cache. Decide for yourself if any difference really exists between these two cases, and if there is a difference, modify the linked list package so that there is not. Then simplify ca_add() by eliminating this check.

4. The function ca_check() is inefficient because it executes a block memory movement (via llretrieve()) before checking each item. This waste could be avoided if we created another function, say llexamine(), which would return a pointer to the current item instead of the item itself. Add this function to the linked list module. Modify ca_check() to use this function.

5. Using the cache package, write and test the code to check for overused words, as originally described. Prove through inspection the validity of the code.

6. Think of two more generic linked list functions. Add them to the linked list module. Prove their correctness through inspection.

7. Eliminate the global variables head, tail, and listlength from the linked list module. Make any modifications necessary to the module so that each function is still covered, albeit inefficiently.

CHAPTER 4 Run Time Context Resolution

4.1. REVIEW

In the previous chapter we saw how to approach a particular problem of data organization as a specific instance of a more general problem. We looked at the process of breaking down a problem into a series of smaller, also general, problems. Throughout this process we focused on two goals of package design. The first was modularity, or the design of packages which are self-contained and clearly defined. The second was reusability, or the design of packages which could be applied to many different programming situations.

We studied the problem of writing a program to detect overused words within a body of text. The software tool needed to solve this problem was a cache-like mechanism which, it turned out, could be developed from a linked list structure.

Linked lists are generally useful mechanisms. We undertook to develop a linked list package which dealt only with the truly generic features of linked lists. The package we developed was therefore reusable. This package had clearly defined primitives. These primitives dealt with a small number of variables and performed a well defined function. Each primitive was fully inspectable, and therefore demonstrably valid.

Using the linked list package we were able to develop a cache package which was both general and modular. This cache package was used to solve our original problem and because it was reusable, we will be ahead of the game the next time we run into a cache problem.

4.2. LIMITATIONS ON OUR LINKED LIST PACKAGE

The implementation of the linked list package has several constraints on its use. To study these constraints, let us consider a new problem. Say, for example, the personnel department of a company maintains a data file that contains personnel job actions in chronological order. Each job action contains a line with a social security number, name, and job action code, which can either be "s" for started, "t" for terminated, or "p" for promoted. The program we will build will read this file and create two output lists, one of current employees, and one of ex-employees. Both lists will be in chronological order.

Each name can appear on only one list. If an ex-employee is rehired, his name should appear on the list at the date on which he was rehired.

A typical input file looks like this

```
055-33-5478 Amy Smith                         s
045-23-5739 John Gold                         s
946-28-5728 Ronald Lender                     s
055-33-5478 Amy Smith                         p
045-23-5739 John Gold                         t
  etc
```

The two output lists created from the typical input file look like this

Current Employees

```
055-33-5478 Amy Smith
946-28-5728 Ronald Lender
etc.
```

Ex Employees

```
045-23-5739 John Gold
etc.
```

We can solve this problem by creating two linked lists, one for current and one for ex-employees. Our program will read through the file, adding new employees to the end of the current employee list and moving terminated employees to the end of the ex-employee list. A bird's eye view of this program looks like this

```
initialize_list(employee_list);
initialize_list(ex_employee_list);

while(read_employee(next_employee) != DONE) {

  if (code(next_employee) == START) {
    if (in_list (next_employee, ex_employee_list))
      remove_from_list (next_employee, ex_employee_list);
    add_to_list (next_employee, employee_list);
  }

  if (code(next_employee) == TERMINATE) {
    remove_from_list (next_employee, employee_list);
    add_to_list (next_employee, ex_employee_list);
  }
}
print_list (employee_list);
print_list (ex_employee_list);
```

Our linked list package from the previous chapter can *almost* serve as the basis for this program. The function initialize_list(), for example, is almost identical to the llinit() function in the package. However, because our linked list package is not exactly what is required to solve this problem, several new issues need to be addressed.

4.3. COMPILE TIME VS RUN TIME DEFINITIONS

Our first stumbling block is concerned with compile time context resolution. As the package is written, the nature of the items stored in the linked list is wired to the package. By wired, we mean defined in the source code. The item descriptions are easy to find because they are neatly packaged into a header file, but the source code will still need changing, and the package will need recompiling. More importantly, the linked list object code is different and incompatible with the linked list object code used for other applications.

This incompatibility is not a serious problem, especially when weighed against recreating the package from scratch. The incompatibility will however create ongoing maintenance headaches. It would be much easier to have a single source code file and a single object code file. Enhancements could then be made transparently to client programs, so long as the enhancements are upwardly compatible.

Our current implementation requires that each client maintain, at the very least, private header file and private object file. This maintenance will usually include a private source file as well, for convenience if nothing else.

All of these similar but slightly different files make centralization of responsibility for package maintenance practically impossible. Each upgrade or bug fix to the linked list module means that new copies must be distributed to all client programmers, and that each new package must be recompiled using its own private header file. This process is difficult to manage reliably and effectively.

A second problem exists which is even more serious—compile time structure definition. Our linked list package is hardwired to a single linked list. No modification of the header file will allow a program to manipulate more than one list using this package. For instance, in the personnel problem, we can use the package to maintain either the current employee list or the ex-employee list, but not both.

By allowing contextual information of a list to be defined at run time, we can create a package that can be maintained as a single source and single object. If the run time context definition is sufficiently robust, we will have a single object file that can be used by any program requiring a linked list. If we can define the structural information of a list at run time, then we will have a package usable for any number of linked lists.

This chapter examines the changes needed to affect run time context resolution. The next chapter examines the issue of run time structure resolution. Later we will see the techniques discussed in these chapters used to achieve run time definition of context and structure applied to other data manipulation packages.

4.4. A CLOSER LOOK AT COMPILE TIME CONTEXT RESOLUTION

The context elements of a linked list are those elements which are application specific. When we developed our linked list package in the previous chapter, we packaged these elements together into a single structure. We defined this structure as itemtype, and placed the definition in a header file (lldef.h) where it could easily be found and modified.

As the linked list module was recompiled, this header file was included and the linked list structure was adjusted to accommodate the application specific information. In the case we examined, the application specific information was a character string. For other applications, it may include other information. If, for example, we were solving our personnel problem using the linked list package (which we know is impossible), lldef.h might look like this

```
struct itemtype {
   char ssnum[12];
   char name[40];
};
```

This structure declaration contains information used by the compiler to allocate memory when and if such a structure is declared to exist. The existence of such a structure is declared by a statement such as

```
struct itemtype item1;
```

The compiler retrieves two pieces of information from the structure type declaration: the memory requirements for such structures and how the memory is to be referenced. In this case, 52 bytes of memory are needed. As for the memory references, the compiler interprets the structure declaration as a set of mappings between symbols, such as struct_name.ssnum[0], and addresses, such as the first byte allocated for the structure.

With these declarations of itemtype and item1, we can use statements such as

```
printf ("Name:%s\n", item1.name);
```

If the compiler has set aside 52 bytes of storage for item1 beginning at Location 1000, this statement is understood as a print request for the string whose starting location is 1013.

4.5. RUN TIME CONTEXT RESOLUTION

To control context resolution at run time, we need to take responsibility away from the compiler both for defining the number of bytes needed for storage and for managing the internal usage of that storage.

Run time memory management can be controlled through the use of the standard functions malloc() and free(). If you recall, malloc() was used in the original linked list packet by llcrlink():

```
struct linktype {
  struct linktype *next;
  struct linktype *previous;
  struct itemtype item;
};



static struct linktype *llcrlink()
{
  return ((struct linktype*)
          malloc(sizeof(struct linktype)));
}
```

When `malloc()` allocates a new link for a list, the number of bytes allocated is the number needed for a structure of type `linktype`. The compiler knows this space is equal to the number of bytes needed for two `linktype` structure pointers plus the number needed for the embedded `itemtype` structure. The latter structure type is defined in the header file, and the value returned by `sizeof()` is resolved at compile time.

To make context run time resolvable, we also need to take responsibility for size determination. We can accomplish this task by adding a new static global variable, `itemlength`, which will contain the number of bytes our particular application wants to store in the linked list. We can also add a new function, `llsetsize()`, to set this variable at run time.

By following the steps just described, the application specific storage structure is taken out of the `linktype` structure definition. Thus, the function `llcrlink()` needs modification to reflect these changes. The following code shows these changes:

```
#include <stdio.h>

struct linktype {
  struct linktype *next;
  struct linktype *previous;
  char *item;
};

static struct linktype *head = NULL;
static struct linktype *tail = NULL;
static struct linktype *clp = NULL;

static int listlength = 0;
static int itemlength = 0;

llsetsize() /* Set storage requirements. */
int size;
{
  itemlength = size;
}
```

```
static struct linktype *llcrlink()
{
  char *malloc();
  struct LINKTYPE *link;
  link = (struct LINKTYPE *)
         malloc(sizeof(struct LINKTYPE));
  link->item = malloc(itemlength);
  return(link);
}
```

Because these changes are typical of a general approach to run time context resolution, they are worth examining in detail at this point.

CHANGE I—REPLACEMENT OF ITEMTYPE

Original version:

```
struct linktype {
  struct linktype *next;
  struct linktype *previous;
  struct itemtype item;
};
```

New version:

```
struct linktype {
  struct linktype *next;
  struct linktype *previous;
  char *item;
};
```

In linktype, the third element, the structure type itemtype was changed to a char *. C has no facility for making the size of structures adjustable at run time. The purpose of the original itemtype was to tell the compiler how much memory was needed for an application specific item. This information is now stored in itemlength, and determined at run time.

Other declarations of type itemtype throughout the packet should be changed accordingly. Modify all routines that accept an item as a parameter, such as lladd():

Original version:

```
lladd(newitem)
struct itemtype *newitem;
```

New version:

```
lladd(newitem)
char *newitem;
```

One word of warning is necessary here. This change assumes a basic similarity in all addresses. Specifically, it assumes that any valid address is a valid character address. The C programming language does not guarantee this assumption and it is possible to imagine architectures in which this assumption is not true. In those environments, some other master address type may be required. It is even possible (but difficult) to imagine environments that do not contain any such master address type. Odd compilers like these may require special handling.

CHANGE II—LOSS OF lldef.h

Original version:

```
/* File: lldeh.h - Modified for Word Caches*/

#define WORDLEN 30
struct itemtype {
  char string[WORDLEN];
};
```

New version: This header file is no longer needed.

In the original, lldef.h contained the definition of itemtype. Without this definition a compiler error would have been generated when we referenced itemtype in the definition of linktype. The first change eliminated this reference and the header file is, for the moment at least, no longer needed.

CHANGE III—ADDITION OF VARIABLE ITEMLENGTH.

The package assumes itemlength contains the number of bytes needed to store the application specific information. This package does not care what is being stored, it cares only about the structural integrity of the list.

CHANGE IV—ADDITION OF FUNCTION llsetsize()

The function llsetsize() is the officially sanctioned method of setting itemlength. By making itemlength a static global variable we can guarantee that all modifications of itemlength go through this approved channel.

The client programmer is responsible for calling this function with the appropriate itemlength before using any other primitives. This responsibility must be clearly documented in the user manual for the package.

CHANGE V—MODIFICATIONS TO llcrlink()

Original version:

```
static struct linktype *llcrlink() /* Allocate space for a link */
{
  return ((struct linktype *)
        malloc(sizeof(struct linktype)));
}
```

New version:

```
static struct linktype *llcrlink()
{
  char *malloc();
  struct LINKTYPE *link;
  link = (struct LINKTYPE *)
         malloc(sizeof(struct LINKTYPE));
  link->item = malloc(itemlength);
  return(link);
}
```

The modifications to llcrlink() are extensive and important enough to warrant a line by line description.

```
struct LINKTYPE *link;
```

A temporary variable called link will contain the address of some memory space yet to be allocated. Eventually this memory space will take the shape of a LINKTYPE. By using link as a handle to this as yet amorphous area, we break the molding of a LINKTYPE into intellectually manageable operations. In other words, we now have a piece of memory called link whose contents are undefined. This situation can be pictured like this

```
link
┌─────┐
│ ??  │
└─────┘
```

The next statement allocates the link:

```
link = (struct LINKTYPE *)
       malloc(sizeof(struct LINKTYPE));
```

The following chronological list documents what is happening in this statement:

1. The sizeof(struct LINKTYPE) is resolved at compile time to be the number of bytes needed to create the structure LINKTYPE. This space will be twice the number of bytes needed to contain the address of a LINKTYPE (one each for next and previous), plus the number of bytes needed for the address of a character.

It is important to note that this issue can be resolved at compile time, *even if we do not know the amount of space needed to store the item itself.* The size of the memory chunk pointed to by item will change depending on the use of the package. However the number of bytes needed to store the address of this memory will always be the same. For the sake of illustration, let us say that two bytes are needed for each address. In this case then, sizeof() resolves to six.

2. The function malloc() is called at run time. It returns the address of the first byte of

of a six byte block of memory which is dynamically allocated. The standard library definitions say that `malloc()` returns a `char *`.

3. The address returned by `malloc()` is typecast so that it can be referred to as the
address of a LINKTYPE. The details of `malloc()` and this typecasting are compiler
specific. This description is conceptual.

4. Now that the LINKTYPE structure has a valid address, we assign the address to
`link`, giving us a handle on this memory. `link` now contains the address of a six byte
block of memory, the contents of which are undefined. Our picture of `link` now looks
like this

link

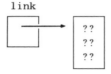

Next we allocate a memory block to contain an application specific item:

```
link->item = malloc(itemlength);
```

Because link contains the address of a structure, we can refer to members of the structure as `link->member_name`. The member `link->item` is the address of the memory area used to store the item in this particular link. The amount of space needed is resolved at run time. It is the current value of `itemlength`, which is set through a call to
`set_length()`.

Let us assume that `itemlength` is set to 10. We now have a temporary variable
`link` pointing to a block of memory containing two undefined pointers, and a third
pointer to another block of memory. This last block is the size of our item, and its contents
are as yet undefined. This `link` story looks like the following

link

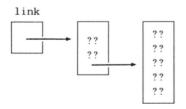

Having allocated space for both the link and its associated item, our function is ready to
return

```
return(link);
```

Thus the contents of `link` are returned. Because `link` contains an address of a now
valid structure LINKTYPE, the calling function can make use of the allocated memory.

Of the 26 bytes of memory allocated, only 2 were initialized. They point to the second memory area.

CHANGE VI—FREEING THE ADDITIONAL MEMORY

The original function `lldelete()` contained this line near the end:

```
free(clp);
```

This line dynamically freed the memory allocated for the link. In the modified versions, two chunks of memory were allocated. Both must now specifically be freed. Our single call to `free()` becomes two calls:

```
free(clp->item);
free(clp);
```

CHANGE VII—MODIFICATIONS TO `moveitem()`

The original package defined a macro called `moveitem()` as such

```
#define moveitem(A,B) movmem(A,B,sizeof(struct itemtype))
```

To make this statement work with run time context definition, it is changed to

```
#define moveitem(A,B) movmem(A,B,itemlength)
```

In the original package `item` was a structure. Actually, `item` was only used when storing or retrieving into the linked list via `moveitem()`. It is now a memory address. References to `item` need to be modified to reflect this change. Each invocation of `moveitem()` should be modified as follows

Old Use:

```
moveitem(newitem, &(clp->item));
```

New Use:

```
moveitem(newitem, clp->item);
```

The standard definition of `movmem()`, or `moveitem()`, says that addresses are expected for both its arguments. `item` is already an address, so this change prevents the address of an address from being passed through.

4.6. OVERVIEW OF CONTEXT MODIFICATIONS

Although many changes seem to have been made to our original linked list package, each was clearly defined and straightforward. The bulk of the code, that large and complex portion dealing with the overall structure and manipulation of the linked list, was unaffected.

The only new testing our package needs is verification that the data are getting in and out of the linked list properly. One valid test would be to rerun our word cache application, making use of the modified linked list package. If it still works, we can assume these new changes are correct.

What new changes are required in our cache routines to interface with our new linked list package? Remarkably, only one minor change is needed. A new function call, `llsetsize()`, needs to be added to set the size of the item being stored in the linked list. Because the cache package was implemented as a fully self-contained package, the high level program using the cache package is completely unaffected.

The call to `llsetsize()` can be inserted, at least for now, in the function which initializes the number of elements allowable in the cache, `setcsize()`. This function is called by the main program before the cache is used. The old version looked like this

```
setcsize(size)
int size;
{
  cachesize = size;
}
```

The new version looks like this

```
setcsize(size)
int size;
{
  cachesize = size;
  llsetsize(sizeof(struct itemtype));
}
```

The reappearance of `itemtype` may seem momentarily confusing; after all, have we not spent this whole chapter eliminating it? The answer is that we have eliminated it, but only from the linked list package. The cache package is still compile time context resolved. We are now at an intermediate state. Our linked list package is more advanced than our cache package. In a later chapter we will apply these same modification techniques to the cache package.

From our program's point of view, the cache packet is used exactly as it has been. In fact this situation can be generalized to a guiding principle of package design.

The Rule of Trickle Up Design Modification

A package should be designed so that latter modifications have at most a minimal effect on packages no more than one level above this package in a calling hierarchy. Packages beyond one level should be completely unaffected.

What have we actually gained from these modifications? The advantage of setting a link size with a function call rather than a header file may not seem obvious, but we have actually made a quantum improvement in our package. We now have a package which is reusable, in the traditional sense of the word. We can compile this package once and link the resulting object code to any program needing a linked list. We can maintain a single source file, and any improvements will be automatically incorporated into any program using this package. Thus, these modifications have many positive implications for large scale, multi-programmer system design.

4.7. EXERCISES

1. In Change IV, the claim is made that "making `itemlength` a static global variable, we can guarantee that all modifications go through this approved channel". How can we be so sure of this?

2. Change VI showed the following addition:

```
free(clp->item);
free(clp);
```

Could these statements be reversed? Why or why not?

3. Look again at the new version of `llcrlink()`.

```
1. static struct linktype *llcrlink()
2. {
3.    char *malloc();
4.    struct LINKTYPE *link;
5.    link = (struct LINKTYPE *)
6.          malloc(sizeof(struct LINKTYPE));
7.    link->item = malloc(itemlength);
8.    return(link);
9. }
```

Answer the following questions.
(a) Why is the function declared `static`?
(b) What does this function return?
(c) Which line number sets aside space for the application specific item to be stored?
(d) Why is `link` declared as a pointer rather than a structure?
(e) How does this routine know how much memory is needed for storing an application specific item?

CHAPTER 5 Run Time Structure Resolution

5.1. LIMITATIONS IN OUR LINKED LIST PACKAGE

Now that we have developed a reusable linked list package, we become victims of our own success. Linked lists are very useful and, with our package, they are easily manipulated. However we are still limited to a single linked list per program, and this limitation implies some further restrictions:

1. Only one package can use the linked list package. If we use a package that is based on the linked list package, we cannot use the linked list package for other purposes.

2. If we use a package that requires the linked list package, we cannot use any other package that requires the linked list package.

These limitations strike at the very foundation of package programming. As users, we should not have to understand the implementation of a package. If we choose to use a cache package, for instance, we should not have to know that the cache is built on top of a linked list package. Yet, because of the package limitations described we are in a situation where we need to be aware of the underlying implementation of the packages before we can plan an overall programming strategy.

The remainder of this chapter deals with removing these limitations. After removal we will have a firm foundation for any and all of the linked list operations that our program may need, one that supports multiple lists, and lists of different types. Such a package will not only be reusable, but universally reusable. In subsequent chapters, we will apply these same techniques to create packages for other data structures, such as caches, queues, and sets.

5.2. ONE SOLUTION: DUPLICATE LINKED LIST MODULES

To start, let us look at a quick fix to the problem of getting support for the two linked lists needed for our personnel management program. We could make a copy of the package and then give it slightly altered function names, for example add an "x" prefix to each name.

We would then have the standard routines `llcrlink()`, `llinit()`, `llhead()`, etc. in the original package, and their analogues `xllcrlink()`, `xllinit()`, `xllhead()`, etc. in the copy. The original routines (without the x prefix) would be called to manipulate the first linked list, and the copied routines (with the x prefix) would be called to manipulate the second linked list. Thus, our pseudocoded problem would change into a program like the following:

```
initialize_list(employee_list);
xinitialize_list(ex_employee_list);
while(read_employee(next_employee) != DONE) {
  if (code(next_employee) == START) {
    if (xin_list (next_employee, ex_employee_list))
       xremove_from_list (next_employee,
       ex_employee_list);
    add_to_list (next_employee, employee_list);
  }

  if (code(next_employee) == TERMINATE) {
    remove_from_list (next_employee, employee_list);
    xadd_to_list (next_employee, ex_employee_list);
  }
}
print_list (employee_list);
xprint_list (ex_employee_list);
```

This approach has several disadvantages which should be apparent. First, we have duplicated a large section of code, changing only external function names. This fix is like writing code to increment any of ten different integer values by creating ten different procedures. Second, we have not solved the underlying problem, which is the limitation on the number of linked lists. Instead we have merely postponed the problem by increasing the limit from one to two.

The goal of the next section is to remove all arbitrary limitations on the number of linked lists manageable with this package. Our current package is hardwired to one linked list. In our modified package, the calling program will be able to declare any number of linked lists, and to declare on the fly the specific list being manipulated at any given time. This is what is meant by run time structure resolution. We want the ability to resolve *at run time* which of several alternate structures is being manipulated.

5.3. ANOTHER LOOK AT THE STRUCTURAL ELEMENTS

The current structure `linktype` is a generic linked list structure modifiable at run time to contain information specific to a particular application. The variables used to keep track of a linked list are found in the header region of the linked list module. They are

```
static struct linktype *head = NULL;
static struct linktype *tail = NULL;
static struct linktype *clp = NULL;

static int listlength = 0;
static int itemlength = 0;
```

We could package these variables together into a single structure of type LINKLIST, and declare the existence of such a structure and a pointer to it with these statements:

```
struct LINKLIST {
  struct linktype *head;
  struct linktype *tail;
  struct linktype *clp;

  int listlength;
  int itemlength;
};

static struct LINKLIST l_list;
static struct LINKLIST *list = &l_list;
```

If we make these changes to the header, we also need to change how these variables are referenced in the module. Looking at the variable head as an example, any code that used to reference head now needs to reference either l_list.head or list->head. So, a line that used to read

```
head = NULL;
```

would now read either

```
l_list.head = NULL;
```

or

```
list->head = NULL;
```

Either of these alterations means changing almost every line of code in the module. However the changes are very straightforward, easily made in most text editors. If we decide to go with the second form, referencing the variables indirectly through the pointer list, then the following changes need to be made throughout the packet:

Old String	New String
head	list→head
tail	list→tail
clp	list→clp
listlength	list→listlength
itemlength	list→itemlength

These changes are essentially style changes and have no effect on the underlying logic of the code. The client/package interface is not altered in the slightest, and the Trickle Up rule of the previous chapter is intact because the packages calling this package are unaffected.

You may be wondering at this point why we are bothering to make these changes. The reason is that we have now embodied within the code our understanding of what it means to create a linked list. There are three independent actions that, taken together, constitute the creation of a linked list:

1. The declaration of the structure LINKLIST defines the concept of a linked list.

2. The declaration of l_list creates an instance of a linked list.

3. The declaration of *list, and the assignment of address of l_list makes the newly created l_list current.

By separating these three actions, we recognize both their independence and interdependence. They are independent because they can take place at completely different times. They are interdependent because we can declare a list active only if a corresponding structure for it has been declared.

We are now close to our goal of a package which allows multiple link lists. For example, with the following minor change, we can create three potential list candidates, the first of which can be made active:

```
struct LINKLIST {
    struct linktype *head;
    struct linktype *tail;
    struct linktype *clp;

    int listlength;
    int itemlength;
};

static struct LINKLIST list1, list2, list3;
static struct LINKLIST *list = &list1;
```

All that remains to make this package universally reusable is to assign the responsibility for creating a linked list to the client instead of the module, and to develop a mechanism for the client to use to inform the package which list he wants manipulated. In other words, the client should now declare his own linked list(s) and tell the linked list package which linked list is currently active.

Remember our goal here is to allow clients to declare their own linked lists, yet fully shield them from the details of the implementation. To accomplish this goal we must move our type definitions of LINKTYPE and LINKLIST into a header file. Resurrect lldef.h for this purpose. It should now look like this

```
struct LINKTYPE {
  struct LINKTYPE *next;
  struct LINKTYPE *previous;
  char *item;
};

struct LINKLIST {
  struct LINKTYPE *head;
  struct LINKTYPE *tail;
  struct LINKTYPE *clp;
  int listlength;
  int itemlength;
};
```

Client programs can now declare linked list(s) like this

```
#include <lldef.h>
struct LINKLIST list1;
```

This procedure is straightforward, easily documented, and requires an absolute minimum of understanding about implementation details on the part of the user. Now all we need is a mechanism for the client to use to tell the linked list package which list is active.

Such a mechanism has at least two alternatives. The first is to create a new function, say llsetlist(), which makes a new list active. That list then remains active until llsetlist() is called again. The second possibility is to modify each function in the package to accept another parameter, the list on which the operation should be performed.

llsetlist() is easily written. We create a static variable, list, as shown earlier. This variable will always point to the currently active linked list, and will be updated through llsetlist(). The same file used by clients to declare a linked list is also included here. Therefore the header region of the linked list module now becomes

```
#include <lldef.h>
static struct LINKLIST *list;
```

The new function to be added to the module is

```
llsetlist(newlist)
struct LINKLIST *newlist;
{
  list = newlist;
}
```

The rest of the code has already been modified to use list, and no further changes are needed. The other possibility—that of modifying each function—is not much more difficult. The function llhead() is typical, and the necessary modifications are illustrated here.

Old Version:

```
static struct LINKLIST *list;
llhead()
{
   list->clp = list->head;
}
```

New Version:

```
llhead(list)
struct LINKLIST *list;
{
   list->clp = list->head;
}
```

With this approach the static variable list is unnecessary because functions are told at invocation which list should be used.

Choosing one of these techniques over the other depends on the expected use of the package. The llsetlist() method is preferred when lists do not change often because client code then needs only to call llsetlist() when the active list changes. In some situations llsetlist() may need to be called so often that it may just be easier to pass the function in the list as a parameter in the first place.

We will use the first technique described. Then at the end of this chapter we will give a new listing of the linked list package with the changes discussed.

Although we are using the llsetlist() approach, be aware of the danger it presents. If your function makes a list current, and then calls another function which may have its own ideas about which list should be current, you will face some interesting problems. Be sure you understand these issues (see Exercises 2 and 3) before starting the next chapter.

5.4. CONTEXT SENSITIVE OPERATIONS BY CONTEXT INDEPENDENT PACKAGES

Sometimes a context independent package, such as our modified linked list package, must interpret or modify data in a context dependent manner. A good example is a scanning function. Scanning a linked list for a particular item is a common need. In our cache package for example, we developed a very inefficient routine to check the cache for an item:

```
ca_check(lookfor)
struct itemtype *lookfor;
{
   struct itemtype lookat;
   int cmpitem();
```

```
    llhead();
    for (;;) {
       llretrieve (&lookat);
       if (cmpitem(lookfor, &lookat)) {
         lldelete();
         lladdhead(&lookat);
         return (1);
       }
       if (!llnext())
         return (0);
    }
}
```

This routine is inefficient because of its use of the function llretrieve(). Before checking a link for the presence of an item, it copies the entire item into the temporary variable (lookat). This extra procedure is an unacceptable price to pay for looking at the contents of a structure.

An alternative is to change

```
if (cmpitem(lookfor, &lookat)) {
```

to

```
if (cmpitem(lookfor, clist.clp->item))
```

This change allows us to perform the comparison while avoiding the memory movement produced with each call to retrieve(). This change however has a major drawback. The client code, the cache module, is now using clist, a structure which is owned by the linked list package. If the linked list implementation changes, this structure could change or even disappear. Client code can *never* make assumptions about how lower level package will be implemented, so a decision is necessary.

Obviously the cache module is caught between a rock and a hard place. Either performance or modularity must be sacrificed. If we choose to use llretrieve(), we pay an unacceptable performance penalty. If we choose to use clist, we pay dearly if the linked list package changes.

There is another issue which is perhaps even more important, functionality responsibility. The cache module is trying to perform a scan on a linked list even though this functionality is a general linked list problem, and as such should be solved in the linked list package.

To generalize the scanning problem and provide a new linked list primitive, say llcheck(), the context specific code must be segregated into a separate function. The client is responsible for providing this application specific function.

The following primitive scans the list looking for a specific item. If the item is found, the clp is set to that link. Either TRUE or FALSE is returned to indicate the success of the search.

```
llcheck(lookfor)
char *lookfor;
{
  for (;;) {
    if (match(list->clp->item, lookfor))
      return (1);
    else
      if (!llnext())
        return (0);
}
```

Obviously, this function also makes assumptions about how the linked list is implemented. But this function is part of the linked list package, and as such has that right. The important point to note is that checking the equality of two items is impossible for a generic linked list package. The concept of equality depends both on the type of information being stored and the context in which it is being referenced. So, the responsibility for determining what it means to ''match'' must rest with the client.

To drive home the point about the application specific nature of equality, consider the two examples of using linked lists already described in this book. For the Word Box problem discussed in Chapter 3, the structure of linked list items looked like the following:

```
struct wordtype {
  char word[40];
};
```

Equality for this application means a string comparison of the only member of the structure:

```
match(item1, item2)
struct wordtype *item1, *item2;
{
  return (!strcmp(item1->word, item2->word));
}
```

For the personnel problem, described earlier in this chapter, items look quite different:

```
struct persontype {
  char ssnum[12];
    char name[40];
  }
```

In this case, equality means a string comparison on only one of the members of the structure:

```
match(item1, item2)
struct persontype *item1, *item2;
{
```

```
    return (!strcmp(item1->ssnum, item2->ssnum));
}
```

For some applications matching means byte by byte equality of the entire item. For others it means string equality, that is byte by byte equality up to and including a null terminator. For others still it means checking specific components of itemtype for arithmetic equality, or perhaps looking for logical relationships between components. In fact, the definition of matching may even change over the course of a program.

   Several mechanisms are available for resolving this context specific function match(). In discussing and pros and cons of each, we will see analogies to other problems dealt with previously in this chapter.

OPTION 1: LINK TIME match() RESOLUTION

The easiest method is to resolve the issue at link time. The applications programmer can link to a module containing an externally available function match(). This function will then be called.

   This situation is very similar to our initial pass at the linked list package, when we created a package hardwired to a single linked list. In that instance, link time resolution meant our match function was hardwired. A programmer choosing from available packages had to know which required match() functions, and had to use no more than one of those packets, either directly or indirectly.

OPTION 2: PASSING IN THE MATCH FUNCTION DURING PROCEDURE CALLS

The C programming language allows the address of a function to be used as a parameter to a function call. Functions such as llcheck() that need to use match() can receive its address as one of their parameters. This solution is common and workable. In the linked list discussions, we proposed a similar method for determining which linked list was being manipulated.

   To demonstrate, this client program declares an application specific matching function called cmpitem() and passes its address as a parameter to the linked list routine llcheck():

```
int cmpitem();
#include <lldef.h>
...
main()
{
  ...
  llcheck(lookfor, cmpitem)
  ...
}
```

The programmer then writes cmpitem():

```
cmpitem(item1, item2)
struct itemtype *item1, *item2;
{
  return (!strcmp(item1->string, item2->string));
}
```

llcheck() is modified to accept this function as a parameter. The new version looks like this

```
llcheck(lookfor, match)
char *lookfor;
int (*match)();
{
  for (;;) {
    if ((*match)(list->clp->item, lookfor))
      return (1);
    else
      if (!llnext())
        return (0);
  }
}
```

OPTION 3: CREATING A llsetmatch() FUNCTION

The third option assumes that at any given time, a linked list can have one associated match function. We add a function llsetmatch() which sets (or changes) the function currently considered match(). From the client's perspective, this option is probably the easiest. A pointer to this function is added to the linked list structure definition in lldef.h:

```
struct LINKLIST {
  struct LINKTYPE *head;
  struct LINKTYPE *tail;
  struct LINKTYPE *clp;
  int listlength;
  int itemlength;
  int (*match)();
};
```

llsetmatch() is added to the linked list packet:

```
llsetmatch(numatch)
int (*numatch)();
{
  list->match = numatch;
{
```

Clients are responsible for using this function to set match currency:

```
int cmpitem();
...
llsetmatch(cmpitem);
```

And finally, functions in the linked list package that need to use this function do so like this

```
llcheck(lookfor)
char *lookfor;
{
  for (;;) {
    if ((*list->match)(list->clp->item, lookfor))
      return (1);
    else
      if (!llnext())
          return (0);
  }
}
```

This chapter has seen many changes to the linked list package. The next two sections show what the package now looks like.

5.5. CURRENT VERSION OF lldef.h

```
struct LINKTYPE {
  struct LINKTYPE *next;
  struct LINKTYPE *previous;
  char *item;
};
struct LINKLIST {
  struct LINKTYPE *head;
  struct LINKTYPE *tail;
  struct LINKTYPE *clp;

  int listlength;
  int itemlength;

  int (*match)();
};
```

5.6. CURRENT VERSION OF LINKED LIST PACKAGE

```c
#include <lldef.h>
#include <stdio.h>

static struct LINKLIST *list;

#define moveitem(A,B)  movmem(A,B,list->itemlength)
/* Use this macro as moveitem(from, to) */

llsetmatch(numatch) /* Set matching function */
int (*numatch) ();
{
  list->match = numatch;
}


/* Set clp to desired link, return True if found, False otherwise */
llcheck(lookfor)
char *lookfor;
{
  for (;;) {
    if ((*list->match)(list->clp->item, lookfor))
        return (1);
    else
        if (!llnext())
            return (0);
  }
}


llsetlist(new_list) /* Set this module to work with a new list. */
struct LINKLIST *new_list;
{
  list = new_list;
}


llsetsize(size) /* Set the storage requirements for the list. */
int size;
{
  list->itemlength = size;
}


static struct LINKTYPE *llcrlink() /* Allocate storage for a link. */
{
```

```
    char *malloc();
    struct LINKTYPE *link;
    link = (struct LINKTYPE *) malloc(sizeof(struct LINKTYPE));
    link->item = malloc(list->itemlength);
    return(link);
}


llinit(newitem) /* Initialize the structure. */
char *newitem;
{
    struct LINKTYPE *llcrlink();

    list->head = list->tail = list->clp = llcrlink();
    list->clp->next = list->clp->previous = NULL;
    moveitem(newitem, list->clp->item);
    list->listlength = 1;
}

llhead() /* Set the CLP to the head of the list. */
{
    list->clp = list->head;
}

lltail() /* Set the CLP to the tail of the list. */
{
    list->clp = list->tail;
}


/* Set the CLP to the next link, return FALSE if at end of list,
    TRUE otherwise. */
llnext()
{
    if (list->clp->next == NULL)
        return (0);
    else {
        list->clp = list->clp->next;
        return (1);
    }
}


/*
Set the CLP to the previous link, return FALSE if at head of list,
TRUE otherwise. */
llprevious()
{
```

```
   if (list->clp->previous == NULL)
      return (0);
   else {
      list->clp = list->clp->previous;
      return (1);
   }
}


llretrieve(newitem)  /* Retrieve the item from the CLP link. */
char *newitem;
{
   moveitem(list->clp->item, newitem);
}


/*
Add a new link containing this item to the link following the CLP,
and reset CLP to new link.  */
lladd(newitem)
char *newitem;
{
   struct LINKTYPE *newlink;
   struct LINKTYPE *llcrlink();

/* Create new link.
   --------------- */
   newlink = llcrlink();
   moveitem(newitem, newlink->item);
   list->listlength++;

/* Reset pointers.
   --------------- */
   newlink->next = list->clp->next;
   newlink->previous = list->clp;
   if (list->tail == list->clp)
      list->tail = newlink;
   else
      list->clp->next->previous = newlink;
   list->clp->next = newlink;
   list->clp = newlink;
}


lladdhead(newitem)  /* Add a new head, reset CLP. */
char *newitem;
{
   struct LINKTYPE *newlink;
   struct LINKTYPE *llcrlink();
```

```
/* If empty, initialize list.
   ------------------------- */
   if (ll_length() == 0) {
      llinit(newitem);
      return;
   }
/* Create new link.
   --------------- */
   newlink = llcrlink();
   moveitem(newitem, newlink->item);
   list->listlength++;

/* Reset pointers.
   -------------- */
   newlink->previous = NULL;
   newlink->next = list->head;
   list->head->previous = newlink;
   list->clp = list->head = newlink;
}

lldelete() /* Delete and free the CLP, reset CLP to head. */
{
   struct LINKTYPE *before, *after;

/* Is this the only link?
   --------------------- */
   if (list->head == list->clp && list->tail == list->clp) {
      list->head = list->tail = NULL;
   }
/* Is this the head?
   ---------------- */
   else if (list->head == list->clp) {
      list->head = list->head->next;
      list->head->previous = NULL;
   }
/* Is this the tail?
   ---------------- */
   else if (list->tail == list->clp) {
      list->tail = list->tail->previous;
      list->tail->next = NULL;
   }
/* Otherwise, it must be inside the list.
   ------------------------------------ */
   else {
      before = list->clp->previous;
      after = list->clp->next;
```

```
      before->next = after;
      after->previous = before;
   }
/* Delete CLP.
   ----------- */
   free(list->clp);
   list->clp = list->head;
   list->listlength--;
}

ll_length() /* Return the length of the list. */
{
   return (list->listlength);
}
```

5.7. EXERCISES

1. Show how a program could use the original linked list package (i.e., as it existed before the modifications described in this chapter) to manipulate two linked lists, where the first is no longer needed by the time the second is initiated.

2. In this chapter we discussed two methods for setting the current list. We chose the method of writing a function llsetlist() to set the current list, a method that will be followed throughout this book. As pointed out, this method is not without its problems. Consider the following function:

```
my_function()
{
   static struct LINKLIST my_list;
   llsetlist(&my_list);
   other_function();
   use_my_list();
}
```

Now suppose other_function() is rewritten at a later date to use a linked list:

```
other_function()
{
   static struct LINKLIST other_list;
   llsetlist(&other_list);
   use_other_list();
}
```

What effect will this rewrite of other_function() have on my_function()? How can my_function() guard against this?

3. This chapter discussed a second method of setting the current list, use of another parameter. Show exactly what changes would have to be made in the functions to implement this method. Modify the code from the previous exercise to use this method. Does this method guard against the problems discussed in Exercise 2? Why or why not?

CHAPTER 6 **Performance**

6.1. REVIEW

In Chapter 2 we showed how to create a modifiable data package applicable to a variety of problems. A linked list package demonstrated this process. This package was further generalized over the course of the next two chapters, and eventually all of the application specific details were made definable at run time. We have discussed the advantages of this style of programming. This chapter discusses the major disadvantage–performance degradation.

Up until now we have been rather dogmatic in insisting that package design be entirely self contained. We made a major concession in Chapter 5 by allowing clients to have access to those structural elements of the linked list necessary to affect run time definitions. In this chapter, we consider relaxing these design requirements even further for the sake of performance.

6.2. MEASURING PERFORMANCE

Most programmers have very few ideas about how their programs spend their time. Without good data, it makes little sense to worry about improving efficiency. As an example, consider measuring the cost of calling `llnext()` in the program that looked for overused text words. `llnext()` was called from the cache function `ca_check()`. The code looked like this

```
ca_check(lookfor)
struct itemtype *lookfor;
{
    struct itemtype lookat;
    cmpitem();

    llhead();
    for (;;) {
        llretrieve (&lookat);
```

```
        if (cmpitem(lookfor, &lookat)) {
          lldelete();
          lladdhead(&lookat);
          return (1);
        }
        if (!llnext())
          return (0);
    }
}
```

If we are going to question the performance of package style programming, this call to
llnext() seems like a likely target. We have added the overhead of a function call and
have replaced what, in many cases, would be code no more complicated than

```
list = list->next;
```

What has this modularization cost us? Many operating system environments have mechanisms available for precise measurements of time passage. Even without such tools, rea-
sonably accurate measurements can be made by writing test programs like the following

```
#include <stdio.h>
#include <lldef.h>
main()
{
    int m1, m2, m3, valu;

    struct LINKLIST l;

/* How many iterations?
   ------------------- */
    printf ("m3: ");
    scanf ("%d", &m3);
    printf ("m3: %d\n", m3);

/* Initialize list.
   --------------- */
    llsetlist(&l);
    llsetsize(sizeof(int));
    llzero();
    valu = 0;

/* Create list with 100 elements.
   ---------------------------- */
    for (m1=0; m1<100; m1++) {
        lladd(&valu);
        valu++;
    }
```

```
/* Read through list once for each iteration.
   ------------------------------------------- */
   printf ("start\n");
   for (m2=0; m2<m3; m2++) {
       llhead();
       for (m1=1; m1<100; m1++) {
           llnext();
       }
   }
   printf ("stop\n");
}
```

This program creates a linked list with 100 links, and then loops through this list m3 times. By modifying the value of m3 at run time, the time necessary to execute a specific number of passes of the list can be measured. Because each pass executes very quickly, m3 should be set high so accurate time measurements can be made.

On one machine, the time between the "start" and "stop" was reproducibly 98 seconds when m3 was 10,000, requiring 1,000,000 invocations of llnext(). We can deduce the llnext() call will take at most 98/1,000,000 seconds, or approximately 0.1 millisecond per call. This guess is an overestimation, because we are not considering the 10,000 calls to llhead(), or the overhead necessary for the two loops.

To find out how much of that 0.1 millisecond is due to package overhead, we can construct a parallel program that accomplishes exactly the same functions with inline code. The difference between the speed of the inline version and the modular version is the packet overhead. The inline version looks like this

```
#include <stdio.h>

struct tlist {
  struct tlist *next;
  struct tlist *previous;
  int valu;
};
static struct tlist *head = NULL, *tail = NULL;
static struct tlist *l1 = NULL, *l2 = NULL;
main()
{
    int m1, m2, m3;
    int more = 1;

/* How many iterations?
   -------------------- */
    printf ("m3: ");
    scanf ("%d", &m3);
    printf ("m3: %d\n", m3);
```

```
/* Initialize list.
   ---------------- */
   head = tail = l1 = (struct tlist *)
                      malloc(sizeof(struct tlist));
   l1->next = l1->previous = NULL;
   l1->valu = 0;

/* Create list with 100 elements.
   ------------------------------ */
   for (m1=1; m1<100; m1++) {
       l2 = (struct tlist *) malloc(sizeof(struct tlist));
       tail = l2;
       l2->next = NULL;
       l2->previous = l1;
       l1->next = l2;
       l2->valu = m1;
       l1 = l2;
   }
/* Read through list once for each iteration.
   ----------------------------------------- */
   printf ("start\n");
   for (m2=0; m2<m3; m2++) {
     l1 = head;
     for (m1=1; m1<100; m1++) {
         l1 = l1->next;
     }
   }
   printf ("stop\n");
}
```

The inline program took 34 seconds between "start" and "stop", indicating approximately 64 seconds of the original 98 was due to package overhead. At first glance, it seems we can significantly enhance program performance by eliminating use of our linked list package. Let us look at the situation in more detail.

To determine the maximum speed for other operations of this program, a test program was written to read a file as quickly as possible. Another program was written to display a file on the terminal as quickly as possible. Measurements were taken of the time taken by these programs to process different sized files. Graphing the time necessary to process a file vs. the size of the file gave these results:

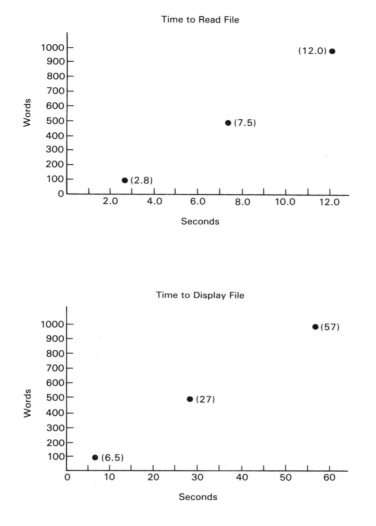

These graphs both intercept the x axis at about 2 seconds, and we will interpret this point as the time necessary to physically open the file. The slopes of these two lines show that it takes approximately 0.055 seconds (55 milliseconds) to display a word, and approximately 0.01 seconds (10 milliseconds) to read it.

Each word needs to be compared against the linked list cache. If the word is found, it is found on average about half-way through the list. If the word is not found, the program must go through the entire list. Also, both types of word must be read (both found and not found words), but only found words are displayed.

The time necessary to process a found word is given by this formula:

```
Time to process one found word =
  time to read word +
  time to process 1/2 cache +
  time to display word +
  file opening overhead
```

The time necessary to process a not found word is a little different. Each word must now search the entire cache, but some savings are realized because the word is not displayed. The formula for a not found word is

```
Time to process one not found word =
  time to read word +
  time to process full cache +
  file opening overhead
```

Consider a file of 1000 words, 25 of which will be found. File overhead accounts for 2000 milliseconds, or 2 milliseconds per word. The time to read and display words has been found to be 10 and 55 milliseconds, respectively. The `llnext()` takes about 0.1 millisecond. The half cache uses about 12 calls, the full cache 25 calls for 1.2 and 2.5 milliseconds, respectively. We can start to substitute actual numbers, and simplify these equations. They become

```
Time to process one found word =
  10 + 1.2 + 55 + 2 = 68.2 milliseconds
```

```
Time to process one not found word =
10 + 2.5 + 2 = 14.5 milliseconds
```

In both cases, the maximum time savings is the time required for `llnext()` during cache operations. The inline test program indicated that about two-thirds of this time could be due to package overhead.

For a found word, this overhead means ⅔ of 1,2 milliseconds, or 0.8 milliseconds. For a not found word, this overhead is ⅔ of 2.5 milliseconds, or 1.7 milliseconds. The savings then is 0.8 out of 68.2, or 1.2% for found words, and 1.7 out of 14.5, or 11.7% for not found words.

We are actually overestimating the value of the savings by not considering the many other contributions to run time. But this analysis tells us that in this typical case, a best case analysis yields an 11.7% reduction in run time for regular words and 1.2% reduction for overused words.

Well and good, you may say, for a cache size of 25. Suppose we had a cache size of 10,000. Would the overhead factor make it worth eliminating the package? Substitution now gives, for found words, a total run time of 1012 milliseconds, 666 of which are `llnext()` overhead.

Our first impression may be that we stand to gain a 65% reduction in run time by eliminating the package overhead. But this is not true. Remember our cache implementation assumed relatively small cache sizes. We would never use a simple linked list to implement a cache of 10,000. Instead we would use a binary tree or a hash table, data concepts described later in this book.

By using a binary tree for example, the time to cache process can be reduced from 1000 milliseconds to something like $\log_2 10000$ llnext() operations $\times$ 0.1 milliseconds per operation, or 1.4 milliseconds. Thus we have far more performance savings than could possibly be realized by eliminating package programming, and we still have all of the advantages of packages.

In fact, even our cache of 25 would benefit from such an implementation. The not found word cache processing becomes $\log_2 25 \times 0.1$, or 0.5 milliseconds per word. Even here we can achieve better performance (14.5% reduction instead of 11.4) by changing the implementation algorithm rather than eliminating the package design.

An important lesson manifests here that you will see again and again in programming:

> Major efficiency gains almost always come from changes in algorithms, not from changes in implementations.

This is a restatement of one of the rules given in Kernighan and Plauger's *The Elements of Programming Style*:

> Don't diddle code to make it faster—find a better algorithm.

6.3. IMPROVING PERFORMANCE

If you are a typical programmer, your reaction to the preceding section will be something like

> All of this is well and fine for MOST programs, by MY programs track incoming enemy missiles and can't afford any extra overhead at all. Therefore package design is really not applicable to my unique kind of work.

We have two answers to these statements. The first is that you are probably wrong. If you go through a thorough analysis of your code similar to the work in the preceding section, you will probably find the numbers simply do not back up your concerns. The second is that if your programs are as important as you think they are, you can afford even less than most to take chances on code that does not absolutely work. Package design is the best tool you have to achieve this guarantee.

The C programming language has one important technique available for improving package performance while making relatively minor concessions to package design. You can use macros to replace function calls with inline code expansion. To see how these macros work, let us look again at the inner loop of our performance testing program.

```
/*Read through list once for each iteration.
  -------------------------------------------- */
   printf ("start\n");
   for (m2=0; m2<m3; m2++) {
       llhead();
       for (m1=1; m1<100; m1++) {
           llnext();
       }
   }
   printf ("stop\n");
```

Without changing our linked list structure, the best we could hope for in performance improvement would be to change the code segment to

```
/* Read through list once for each iteration.
   -------------------------------------------- */
   printf ("start\n");
   for (m2=0; m2<m3; m2++) {
       list->clp = list->head;
       for (m1=1; m1<100; m1++) {
           list->clp = list->clp->next;
       }
   }
   printf ("stop\n");
```

If we try to make this change, we find that our program is not aware of the variable list. We need to make two changes in the package. The first is in the global variable region of the package. We need to change the declaration of list by removing the static declaration. Second, we need to add this statement to the header of our test:

```
extern struct LINKLIST *list;
```

If we run the program with these changes, we will find that the runtime between "start" and "stop" for an m3 of 10,000 is reduced from 98 seconds to 39 seconds. This time is close to the 34 second minimum predicted by the test program earlier in this chapter. Our problem is that we have violated our most important principle of package design—we have forced our client to understand package implementation details.

We can achieve these savings with only minimal violation of our rule by the judicious use of macros. We can create another file, say ll_xpnd.h, which redefines functions by their equivalent inline code expansion. For example, llhead() and llnext() would be given by

```
#define llhead() (list->clp = list->head)

#define llnext() ((list->clp->next == NULL) ? 0 : \
           (list->clp = list->clp->next)))
```

If we modify our test program, changing the header to

```
#include <stdio.h>
#include <lldef.h>
#include <ll_xpnd.h>

extern struct LINKLIST *list;
```

we find the runtime decreases from 98 seconds to 59 seconds.

We still have not achieved our 39 second goal because of the complexity of the #define for llnext(). This definition preserves the original return value from llnext(), even though in this case it is not needed. By adding a new function and corresponding inline definition called llnrnext(), for next with no return, we can simplify the definition to

```
#define llnrnext() (list->clp = list->clp->next)
```

If we change the llnext() call in the test code to a llnrnext() call and #include ll_xpnd.h, we find that the run time indeed decreases to 39 seconds. The difference between 39 and 34 seconds is due to the extra pointer (list). This difference is, even with incoming enemy missiles, acceptable.

We should be aware of what we have traded for this capability. Before, our program could use this package with just these statements:

```
#include <lldef.h>
struct LINKLIST *l;
```

We have now upped the requirements to

```
#include <lldef.h>
#include <ll_xpnd.h>
extern struct LINKLIST *list;
struct LINKLIST *l;
```

We have also introduced a global variable, which is always dangerous. In most cases, this cost is probably too high and we are better off leaving the package as we originally designed it. But in those very few cases where the speed will make an important overall difference, we do have this capability as an ace in the hole.

6.4. EXERCISES

1. In this section, we considered program run time. On a multi-user system, we may be more interested in CPU cycles than run time. Qualitatively, how would a similar analysis of CPU cycles perform?

2. Define inline code expansions for these functions:

```
lltail()
llprevious()
llexamine()
```

3. In the original benchmark program, six linked list manipulation functions were used. If we run this program entering 100,000 for m3, how many times are each of these functions invoked? For each function, take an educated guess as to what percentage of the run time it uses, choosing either
   (a) less than 0.5%
   (b) 0.5 - 1%
   (c) 1 - 10%
   (d) more than 10%

Justify your answers.

CHAPTER 7 **More on Linked Lists**

We have discussed the principals of reusable, verifiable data manipulation packages. Generic linked list primitives were created in Chapter 3 and refined in subsequent chapters. Chapter 6 discussed the reconciling performance and modularity. This chapter gives some more examples of linked list applications using our set of primitives. The remaining chapters will examine primitive sets for other data structures, will implement each as a generic package, and will discuss applications.

7.1. PERSONNEL PROBLEM

A personnel application that seemed suited to a linked list solution was described in Chapter 4. The linked list package was too limited at that time to be of much help. It had no provision for multiple linked lists and called for the maintenance of application specific binaries, thus complicating the programming process. These issues were addressed and corrected in the next two chapters, resulting in a much more robust module.

We can now return to our original problem, which was to interpret a file containing social security numbers, names, and personnel action codes. A typical file might look like this

```
055-33-5478 Amy Smith        s
045-23-5739 John Gold        s
946-28-5728 Ronald Lender    s
055-33-5478 Amy Smith        p
045-23-5739 John Gold        t
  etc
```

The program is to read this input file and create a report. The first part of the report is to list the current employees of the company. The second part is to list employees who have left the company. Both parts will reflect the chronological order of the input file. A sample report created from the above input file might look like this

```
Current Employees

055-33-5478 Amy Smith
946-28-5728 Ronald Lender
etc.

Ex-Employees

045-23-5739 John Gold
etc.
```

As we discussed, this problem can be solved by creating two linked lists, one for current employees and one for ex-employees. As we read through the input file, we take the following steps when encountering a hire status code:

1. Determine if the person is in the ex-employee list.
2. If he is, delete him from the ex-employee list.
3. Add him to the current employee list.

When encountering a terminated status code:

1. Determine if the person is in the employee list.
2. If she is, delete her from the employee list
3. Add her to the ex-employee list.

A trace of the two linked lists shows how each list changes as new lines are read from the input file:

```
Amy Smith      055-33-5478 s
John Gold      045-23-5739 s
Ronald Lender  946-28-5728 s

Current:
Amy Smith    ---    John Gold ---- Ronald Lender
055-33-5478         045-23-5739    946-28-5728

Ex:
NULL
       . . . . . . . . . . . . . . . . . . . . . . . . . . . . . . . . . . . . . .

Amy Smith      055-33-5478 p
```

This has no effect, because "p" is not a recognized action code.

```
       . . . . . . . . . . . . . . . . . . . . . . . . . . . . . . . . . . . . . .
```

```
John Gold      045-23-5739  t
```

```
Current:
Amy Smith    ---    Ronald Lender
055-33-5478         946-28-5728
```

```
Ex:
John Gold
045-23-5739
```

The linked lists help track two important pieces of information on each employee—the status of an employee and the seniority of the employee (relative to other employees). Seniority can be determined from an employee's position within a list. The most senior employee is always at the head of the current employee list: the most recent hire at the tail. Similarly, the head and the tail of the ex-employee list contain the first and last termination, respectively. The pseudocode solution to this problem, repeated from before, follows. The program is called emp().

```
emp()
{
  initialize_list(employee_list);
  initialize_list(ex_employee_list);

  while(read_employee(next_employee) != DONE) {

    if (code(next_employee) == START) {
      if (in_list (next_employee, ex_employee_list))
         remove_from_list (next_employee, ex_employee_list);
      add_to_list (next_employee, employee_list);
    }

    if (code(next_employee) == TERMINATE) {
      remove_from_list (next_employee, employee_list);
      add_to_list (next_employee, ex_employee_list);
    }
  }
  print_list (employee_list);
  print_list (ex_employee_list);
}
```

It is clear employee_list and ex_employee_list are of type LINKLIST, but we run into trouble when trying to interpret the pseudofunction initialize_list(). The linked list primitive function llinit() seems similar, but unlike initialize_list(), requires an item with which to initialize. In other words, llinit() is used to create a new list with exactly one item in it, while initialize_list() is used to create a new list with zero items in it.

We could implement `initialize_list()` with our existing functions by calling `llinit()` and then immediately calling `lldelete()`, effectively setting up a new list with zero items. However, the need to create a new list with zero items seems common, and the more general approach would be to add another primitive to the module (or request an addition from the maintainer). We could call the new primitive `llzero()`.

```
llzero()
{
  list->head = list->tail = list->clp = NULL;
  list->listlength = 0;
}
```

With this modification, we can complete the expansion of pseudocode. Three files are involved. An overview of their structures follows

> File: LLDEF.H
> Generic Linked List Definitions
> File: LL.CC
> Static pointer to current list
> Macro Definitions
> Linked List Functions
> File: EMP.CC
> Application specific structure definitions
> Constant definitions
> cmpemp() definition
> iemplist() definition
> read_employee() definition
> reorg() definition
> main() definition

The global definitions regions of emp.cc contains the definition of an employee type and a few constant definitions. The global region of emp.cc is illustrated as follows. Note that the structure emptype is the application specific information to be stored and manipulated by the linked list package.

```
#include <stdio.h>
#include "lldef.h"

struct emptype {
  char ssnum[12];   /* Employee's social security number.  */
  char name[40];    /* Employee's name.                    */
};
#define DONE NULL
#define START 's'      /* Action code for starting work.    */
#define TERMINATE 't'  /* Action code for terminating work. */
```

The rules for using the linked list package stipulate that calls to `llcheck()`, which scan the list looking for a particular item, must be preceded by a definition of an application specific `match()` function. This program uses `llcheck()` to find specific employees. Two employees are considered identical if their social security numbers match. The function to match employees on the basis of social security numbers is `cmpemp()`.

```
cmpemp(emp1, emp2) /* See if two employees are the same person. */
struct emptype *emp1, *emp2;
{
  return (!strcmp(emp1->ssnum, emp2->ssnum));
}
```

Before using a linked list, both the match function and the item length must be made known to the linked list package. These variables are the same for both the employee and ex-employee lists. One function, `iemplist()` can handle initialization of either list.

```
iemplist(emplist) /* Initialize a linked list of employees. */
struct LINKLIST *emplist;
{
    int cmpemp();          /* This routine was already defined.   */
    llsetlist(emplist); /* Set the list we want to initialize. */

    llzero();              /* Set to empty.                        */
    llsetmatch(cmpemp); /* Define the match function.            */
    llsetsize(sizeof(struct emptype));
                   /* Define the list as a list of employees. */
}
```

The function `rdemp()` reads a line from the input file and apportions the data into an `emptype` structure, whose address is returned. The personnel action code is also returned as a parameter. This function is left as an exercise.

As the pseudocode shows, the actions taken up on encountering START are the same as the actions taken at TERMINATE. In each case

1. See if the employee is in the opposing list.
2. If he is, delete him.
3. Add him to the current list.

The only difference between START and TERMINATE is the designation of which list is opposing and which is current. Both actions can therefore be collapsed into a single function `reorg()` with the lists passed as arguments:

```
reorg(oldlist, newlist, emp) /* Reorganize two lists. */
struct LINKLIST *oldlist, *newlist;
struct emptype *emp;
{
/* Delete from old list if necessary.
   -------------------------------- */
   llsetlist(oldlist);
   llhead();
   if (llcheck(emp))
      lldelete();

/* Add to new list.
   ---------------- */
   llsetlist(newlist);
   if (ll_length() == 0)
      llinit(emp);
   else {
      lltail();
      lladd(emp);
   }
}
```

With these functions in place, the remainder is straightforward.

```
main()
{
   struct LINKLIST curemp, exemp;
   struct emptype *emp;
   char code;
   struct emptype *rdemp();

/* Initialize lists.
   ---------------- */
   iemplist(&curemp);
   iemplist(&exemp);

/* Read through file.
   ----------------- */
   while((emp = rdemp(&code)) != DONE) {

/*    Reorganize lists.
      ---------------- */
      if (code == START)
         reorg(&exemp, &curemp, emp);
      if (code == TERMINATE)
         reorg(&curemp, &exemp, emp);
   }
```

```
/* Print results.
   -------------- */
   printf ("Employees:\n");
   prlist (&curemp);
   printf ("\nEx-Employees:\n");
   prlist (&exemp);
}
```

Multiple linked lists are often useful for categorizing items. Each list represents a separate category. Placement on a list represents some relative status. This employee application is such an application. The category of an employee (current or ex-) is indicated by which list she is on. In other words, list position indicates relative seniority on a list.

Similar problems often exist in multi-user operating systems. Consider coordinating many programs running and sharing a single set of computer resources. Each program must be represented by a structure which includes information such as the memory occupied by the program, the state of the computer when this program last ran, and more.

One linked list, the *active* list, holds all programs currently competing for system resources. Another list, the *wait* list, holds all programs waiting for some system event to occur, such as the completion of an I/O operation. When a program is in such a wait state, it is taken out of competition for system resources.

When a system event occurs, such as the completion of a disk I/O operation, each program on the wait list is checked to see if the event is the anticipated event. If so, the program matched is placed back on the active list. As you can see, the code required to coordinate the wait and active lists would be similar to our personnel solution.

7.2. MEMORY MANAGEMENT

A dynamic memory managing package makes another good example of a linked list application. A dynamic memory manager consists of two externally available procedures, mmget() and mmfree(), which have functions similar to the standard C procedures malloc() and free(). The one difference between our functions and the standard functions is that our procedures will be set up to efficiently collect the garbage. To illustrate a situation where garbage collection could be important, consider this program

```
main()
{
   char *malloc(), *p1, *p2, *p3, *p4, *p5;

   p1 = malloc(1000);      p2 = malloc(1000);
   p3 = malloc(1000);      p4 = malloc(1000);

   free(p1);
   free(p3);

   p5 = malloc(1200);
}
```

Although the implementations of malloc() and free() are compiler dependent, we can consider a hypothetical environment in which malloc() and free() have at their disposal 4500 memory bytes starting at absolute address 1000. This memory block is the *dynamic memory pool*, and, in this case, includes the absolute locations 1000-5500. The statement

```
p1 = malloc(1000);
```

causes malloc() to perform the following

1. Search the dynamic memory pool for the first available block of memory of 1000 bytes. This block is found at locations 1000-2000.

2. "Mark" this block as unavailable.

3. Return the address of the first byte of the block, which is 1000.

When the first four calls to malloc() have been processed, the dynamic memory pool looks like this

```
locations 1000-1999 are used
locations 2000-2999 are used
locations 3000-3999 are used
locations 4000-4999 are used
locations 5000-5500 are free
```

The standard function free() is the reverse of malloc(). It receives a pointer to one of the blocks in the dynamic memory pool previously allocated by malloc(). The pool is first scanned to validate the pointer, and then the block is released for use.

When our sample program finishes the two calls to free(), the dynamic memory pool looks like this

```
locations 1000-1999 are free
locations 2000-2999 are used
locations 3000-3999 are free
locations 4000-4999 are used
locations 5000-5500 are free
```

Notice that the *total* amount of free memory in the dynamic memory pool is 2500 bytes, but the call

```
p1 = malloc(1200)
```

will fail, because there are no more than 1000 bytes available in any one block. Our functions mmget() and mmfree() can solve this problem by dynamically collecting free memory into a single contiguous chunk.

Most important, dynamic memory collection will be kept invisible from our clients, the programs using the dynamically allocated memory blocks. In other words, if a program uses `mmget()` to set a pointer `p1` to a block of memory, `p1` will always point to the same values. Any dynamic memory collection that results in relocating the memory block also results in an automatic update of `p1`. Consider the following sequence of events:

```
mmget (&p1, 5);
mmget (&p2, 5);
mmget (&p3, 5);
```

These three statements result in this dynamic memory pool:

```
locations 1000-1004 are used
locations 1005-1009 are used
locations 1010-1014 are used
locations 1015-5500 are free
```

When we start to use this memory, we see the following:

```
strcpy (p1, 'abcd');
strcpy (p2, 'efgh');
strcpy (p3, 'ijkl');

locations 1000-1004 are used
  They contain: 'abcd'
  p1 contains 1000

locations 1005-1009 are used
  They contain: 'efgh'
  p2 contains 1005

locations 1010-1014 are used
  They contain: 'ijkl'
  p3 contains 1010

locations 1010-5500 are free
```

If we free one of these pointers, the dynamic memory pool is updated to

```
mmfree (p2);

locations 1000-1004 are used
locations 1005-1009 are free
locations 1010-1014 are used
locations 1015-5500 are free
```

If the Dynamic Memory Manager decides to collect garbage and consolidate locations 1005-1009 and 1015-5500, the contents of `p1` and `p3` *must* be updated so that they still point at the strings abcd and ijkl, respectively. When all garbage is collected, we should have this situation:

```
locations 1000-1004 are used
  They contain: 'abcd'
  p1 contains 1000

locations 1005-1009 are used
  They contain: 'ijkl'
  p3 contains 1005


locations 1010-5000 are free
```

Three procedures will be visible to the user in our Dynamic Memory Manager: mmget(), mmfree(), and mmcollect(). An example of a program using these procedures looks like

```
char *pntr;          /* Pointer to the start of a block of memory. */
int nbytes;          /* Number of bytes desired.                   */
int mmget();         /* Procedure to get a block of memory.        */
int mmfree();        /* Procedure to free a block of memory.       */
int mmcollect();     /* Procedure to garbage collect memory.       */
...
mmget(&pntr, nbytes);
...
mmfree(pntr);
mmcollect();
```

The Dynamic Memory Manager uses a linked list to keep track of information about the Dynamic Memory Pool. Each block in the pool is described by one link. The representation of memory is shown in the following illustration.

The calling sequence

```
mmget(&p1, 10);
mmget(&p2, 20);
mmget(&p3, 25);
mmfree(p2);
```

produces this linked list:

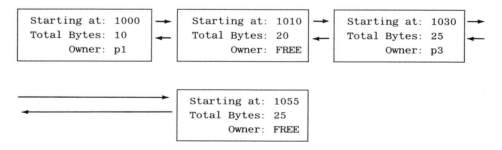

One module, mem.cc, contains all Dynamic Memory Manager functions. The beginning of the module contains the global definitions and variables. The linked list mem of memory_type structures keeps track of which pieces of the dynamic memory pool have been allocated, and to whom. The beginning of the module looks like this

```
/* MEM.CC */
#include <stdio.h>
#include "lldef.h"
#define MEMLEN 4500   /* Bytes in Dynamic Memory Pool.   */
#define USED 'U'       /* Code for a used block.          */
#define FREE 'F'       /* Code for a free block.          */

struct memory_type { /* One block from the Dynamic Pool.  */
  char type;          /* Is this block USED or FREE?       */
  char *start;        /* First byte of the block.          */
  int nbytes;         /* Number of bytes in the block.     */
  char **addr_owner;  /* Address of the pointer passed in. */
};
static char *memstart;       /* Start of dynamic memory pool.   */
static struct LINKLIST mem;  /* List describing status of Pool. */
```

The member addr_owner of the structure memory_type deserves special discussion. This variable keeps track of the address of the pointer to this memory block. The pointer itself resides in the user code. We need to know the address of the pointer so that if the memory pointed to becomes shifted in the course of garbage collection, the pointer itself can be updated, unbeknownst to the client code. The following illustrates the effect of memory shifting.

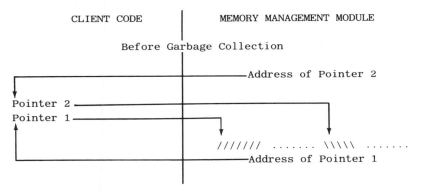

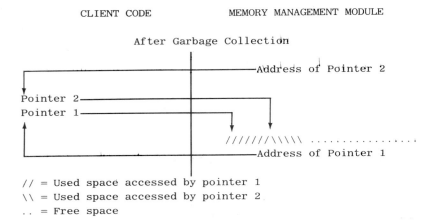

```
// = Used space accessed by pointer 1
\\ = Used space accessed by pointer 2
.. = Free space
```

Because the linked list function llcheck() will be used to find both an available free block in the list and a particular used block, we need to define two separate match() functions—chkfree() and chkused(). They are declared static because they are referenced by name only inside this module (although they are referenced by address inside of ll.c).

```
static int chkfree(ll_item, sample)    /* Find free block. */
struct memory_type *ll_item, *sample;
{
    if ((sample->nbytes <= ll_item->nbytes) &&
        (ll_item->type == FREE))
      return (1);
    else return (0);
}
static int chkused(ll_item, sample) /* Find used block. */
struct memory_type *ll_item, *sample;
{
    if (ll_item->start == sample->start) return(1);
    else return (0);
}
```

The function init(), also static, has several responsibilities. It initializes the linked list structure, allocates memory for the dynamic memory pool, and declares the pool to be a single free block.

```
static init()
{
    struct memory_type sample;
    char *malloc();

/* Initialize linked list structure.
-------------------------------- */
    llsetlist(&mem);
    llsetsize(sizeof(struct memory_type));
```

```
/* Initialize memory.
   ------------------
   memstart = malloc(MEMLEN);

/* Initialize the list with one big free block.
   --------------------------------------------- */
   sample.start = memstart;
   sample.nbytes = MEMLEN;
   sample.type = FREE;
   sample.addr_owner = 0;
   llinit(&sample);
}
```

The static functions `setfree()` and `consolidate()` perform the work of freeing a used memory block. When a block is freed, it is consolidated with adjacent free blocks, if any, so that we do not end up with small pieces of free space next to each other. This kind of rudimentary garbage collection could be accomplished by the standard C library function `free()` as well.

```
static consolidate(first, second)
struct memory_type *first, *second;
{
    first->nbytes += second->nbytes;      /* Consolidate sizes.  */
    first->start =                        /* See which is first. */
        (first->start < second->start) ?
        (first->start) : (second->start);
}
static setfree()
{
struct memory_type *free, *other;

/* Prepare current block for freedom.
   ---------------------------------- */
   free = llexamine();       /* See which block is current, */
   free->addr_owner = 0;     /* Note that block is unowned... */
   free->type = FREE;        /* ... and available for use.   */

/* If previous block is also free, consolidate.
   -------------------------------------------- */
   if (!llishead()) {            /* Don't go beyond head.     */
      llprevious();             /* Check the previous block. */
      other = llexamine();
      if (other->type == FREE) {  /* If free, consolidate.    */
         consolidate(free, other);
         lldelete();
      }
      llnext();                  /* Reset current block.      */
   }
```

```
/* If next block is also free, consolidate.
   --------------------------------------- */
   if (!llistail()) {                    /* Don't go beyond tail.    */
      llnext();                          /* Check the next block.    */
      other = llexamine();
      if (other->type == FREE) {         /* If free, consolidate.    */
         consolidate(free, other);
         lldelete();
      }
   }
}
```

Finally we add the three functions that are user-visible to the packet. The function mmget() searches for the first free piece of memory of adequate size, and marks the block as being in use.

```
mmget(addr_owner, nbytes) /* Get a chunk of free space */
char **addr_owner;
int nbytes;
{
   struct memory_type used, free;
   static chkfree(), init();
   static int firsttime = 1;   /* Have we initialized yet? */

/* If this is the first call, initialize dynamic memory pool.
   -------------------------------------------------------- */
   if (firsttime) init();
   firsttime = 0;

/* Find first largest piece of free space.
   --------------------------------------- */
   llhead();                   /* Start search at head of list.    */
   llsetmatch(chkfree);        /* Look for first block large enough.*/
   used.nbytes = nbytes;       /* Definition of large enough.      */
   llcheck(&used);

/* Split block, and make the first part "used".
   ------------------------------------------- */
   llretrieve(&free);
   *addr_owner = free.start;   /* Set user's pointer. */
   used.start = free.start;    /* Set start of block. */
   used.type = USED;           /* Mark block as used. */
   used.addr_owner = addr_owner;/* Note owner of block.*/
```

```
/* Whatever is left of the block is still "free".
   --------------------------------------------- */
   free.start += nbytes;
   free.nbytes -= nbytes;

/* Replace the old block by the two new ones.
   ---------------------------------------- */
   llreplace(&used);        /* The first part is now in use.   */
   lladd(&free);            /* This is whatever was not needed. */
}
```

The function mmfree() finds the used block being freed, marks it as available, and consolidates it with any adjacent free pieces.

```
mmfree(location)
char *location;
{
    struct memory_type used;
    static chkused(), setfree();

    llhead();                /* Start looking at beginning.    */
    llsetmatch(chkused);     /* Look for a used piece...       */
    used.start = location;   /* ... starting at this location. */
    if (!llcheck(&used))     /* If it isn't there...           */
       return (0);           /* ... return error code.         */
    setfree();               /* Set the place free.            */
    return (1);              /* Return all ok code.            */
}
```

The final user-visible function is mmcollect(), which is, in the end, all that distinguishes these routines from malloc() and free(). All free space is consolidated at the tail of a list. The nature of this algorithm guarantees the tail is always a free block.

```
mmcollect()
{
struct memory_type *next, *llexamine();
int freemem;    /* Counter for total free bytes.                   */
char *nxtslot; /* Slot that a block of memory will be moved to. */

/* Consolidate free space.
   ---------------------- */
   freemem = 0;               /* Initialize number of free bytes. */
   llhead();                  /* Start looking at head.           */
   while (!llistail()) {      /* Examine a block of memory.       */
     next = llexamine();
     if (next->type == FREE) {    /* If this block is free...     */
        freemem += next->nbytes;  /* ...add to free bytes counter*/
        lldelete();               /* ...and delete this block.    */
     }
     else llnext();
   }
```

```
   next = llexamine();              /* Consolidate into the tail.  */
   next->nbytes += freemem;

/* Consolidate used space.
   ---------------------- */
   llhead();                        /* Start at head of the list.    */
   nxtslot = memstart;              /* Get ready to move this block. */
   next = llexamine();              /* The block that will be moved. */
   while (next->type == USED) {     /* If this block is used...      */
     movmem(next->start, nxtslot, next->nbytes);   /* Move it.       */
     next->start = nxtslot;         /* Prepare to move next block... */
     nxtslot += next->nbytes;       /* ...right behind this one.     */
     llnext();
     next = llexamine();
   }
/* Update last block of free space.
   ------------------------------ */
   next->start = nxtslot;
}
```

7.3. EXERCISES

1. Write the functions prlist() and rdemp() for the employee program.

2. The employee program is a good example of a linked list application which can be supported by our package. A two-way linked list is the type implemented in the linked list module. Unlike a two-way linked list, links in a one-way list do not contain pointers to previous links. Therefore you can move only in a single direction, towards the tail. The employee program never executes the previous() command, and pays a performance penalty for unnecessarily maintaining the previous pointer.

   Create another version of the linked list package using a struct definition for a one-way list. This new version should look exactly like the two-way package, so the switch can be made at link time. Update all appropriate functions (or macro definitions). Document those functions no longer supported.

3. Write a Memory Tracing Procedure that can be called to show the status of the dynamic memory pool.

4. Add the function mmstat() to the Dynamic Memory Manager. This function must return two values. The first value must show the total amount of memory available in the pool. The second value must show the largest piece of memory available. This function can be used to determine if the time has come to call mmcollect(). Write this function without scanning the list, modifying existing functions as necessary.

5. Modify mmfree() so that a full garbage collection is always performed with each call. What are the advantages and disadvantages of this change?

6. Modify mmfree() so that garbage is collected whenever the largest single chunk of available memory is less than ¾ of the total available pool.

7. What are the implicit guarantees and limitations of mmget() and mmfree()? What are the potential problems in this code:

```
mmget(&p1, 27);
p2 = p1;
strcpy(p2, 'abcdefghijklmnopqrstuvwxyz');
. . .
printf ("String: %s", p2);
mmfree(p2);
```

Do these problems exist for malloc() and free() as well?

8. What is the essential difference between malloc() and mmget(), which allows mmcollect() to collect garbage? Why is it that the standard routine free() can never be modified to have this capability?

9. The function mmfree() validates its parameter by looking for a used block starting with the same address as the pointer passed in. This validation should also be done by free(). Modify mmfree() to verify that the pointer is actually identical to one of those passed in to mmget(). This verification would guard against the kind of problems described in Problem 7. Why could free() never be changed to make this kind of check, and why would there be no reason to make the change?

10. With some changes, the basic logic of the Dynamic Memory Manager could be used to allocate free space on a disk. Consider these similarities:
Using the Dynamic Memory manager as a model, write a Dynamic Disk Space Allocator which would be responsible for disk space in a file called records.data.

Memory Manager	Disk Space Manager
Initialize Memory for the Dynamic Pool.	Write out blank records to a file.
Find a free block of memory.	Find enough space on the disk for a record.
Assign a block of memory to a pointer.	Assign a block of disk space to a record ID.
Free a block of memory.	Mark a record as having been deleted and make the space available.
Collect all free memory into one contiguous block.	Collect all deleted records into one contiguous block of disk space.

Using the Dynamic Memory manager as a model, write a Dynamic Disk Space Allocator which would be responsible for disk space in a file called records.data.

CHAPTER 8 **Caches Revisited**

Let us consider a common problem, managing disk I/O. In particular, consider writing `readchar()` which is to read a specific character from a disk file. We are given an operating system routine, `readblock()`, which transfers one block of data from a physical disk block to a user buffer. The size of a disk block is operating system dependent, but a typical block could be 1024 bytes in length. The definitions of these two routines, `readchar()`, which we are to write, and `readblock()`, which we have, are these

```
char readchar(file_pntr, char_num)
FILE *file_pntr;        /* Which file to read from. */
long int char_num;      /* Which character to read. */


readblock(file_pntr, block_num, buffer)
FILE *file_pntr;    /* Which file to read from.            */
long block_num;     /* Which physical block to read from.  */
char *buffer;       /* 1024 byte buffer to copy block to.  */
```

Implementing `readchar()` from `readblock()` is no problem. We calculate which disk block contains the requested character and where in the block the character resides. For example, assuming characters and blocks are numbered from zero, the following mappings exist

Character number	Block number	Offset within block
3	0	3
1023	0	1023
1024	1	0
2047	1	1023
2049	2	1

88

Our function `readchar()` calls `readblock()` to read the appropriate disk block, and `readchar()` returns the character at the appropriate offset within that block.

These actions sound simple enough, but let us consider the performance of our `readchar()`. How is this routine likely to be used? A typical client program for `readchar()` will probably look something like this

```
for(n=0; n<=1000; n++) {
  string[index++] = readchar(input, n);
}
```

The client code is using our `readchar()` to read 1000 consecutive characters from the input file. We said that a disk block contains 1024 bytes, so these characters span at most two disk blocks. If every call to `readchar()` initiates a physical disk I/O, we will be reading the same disk block over and over again, as many as 1000 times before the client's string is filled. Disk I/O is always slow. This version of `readchar()` will have miserable performance.

A much more efficient algorithm would have us save the disk block before returning. Each call would first check to see if the needed block is already in memory, and if so, avoid the unnecessary and costly disk read.

As long as we are saving the last disk block read, why not save the last two, or even ten? There is always a chance that one of these blocks will be needed again. The more blocks we save, the greater our chances of avoiding a costly disk I/O operation. Of course, the more blocks we save, the greater our memory demands will be also.

However many blocks we decide to save, we would eventually read one block too many. Then we would have to reuse the memory space occupied by one of the blocks. Which block should be thrown away? The best block to discard is the block we would least likely want again.

Choosing which block we are least likely to want again is not an easy task. One common algorithm is to discard the buffer least recently referenced, on the theory that if it has not been used for awhile, it probably will not be used in the near future. Least recently referenced is not the same as oldest. A block may have been read a long time ago, but used recently. If so, it may be used again, and should be kept.

This discussion should sound somewhat familiar. The underlying algorithm was also used to solve the overused words problem of Chapter 3. The underlying data structure, a cache, is also similar, differing only in the application specific information being manipulated. In Chapter 3, our caches contained character strings. Now they contain disk blocks. With luck, some of our existing code can be recycled.

We could incorporate the cache directly into our `readchar()` function, but a more general and testable solution is to create a new software layer that resides between `readchar()` and the low level `readblock()`. We will call this new function `get_block()`. Its function will be to cache I/O buffers and read a physical disk block only when necessary. Overall, our software layers will look like this client software

    Asks for a specific character

readchar ()

    Translates character to block
    and character offset. The block
    is requested from . . .

get_block ()

    which sees if requested block is in
    cache, and if not, calls . . .

readblock ()

    which physically reads the block
    from disk

8.1. OUR EXISTING CACHE PACKAGE

At the end of Chapter 3 application specific information was still hard coded into the
linked list package, albeit neatly packaged into the lldef.h file. To use such a package,
clients would have to maintain different codes for different applications, clearly an ar-
chaic situation by the standards of Chapter 8. Further, a given client program would be
limited to a single linked list per program. Because this limited package was used as the
basis for the cache package, a single program could use, at most, one hard coded cache.
At that time lldef.h file looked like this

```
/* lldef.h */
#define WORDLEN 30
struct itemtype {
  char string[WORDLEN];
};
```

It is worth reviewing the cache module as it was, and seeing exactly which sections of
code caused these limitations. The first few lines of the cache module caused the major
problem with the entire module. Without an internal pointer to the current cache, we were
dependent on the linked list module to maintain cache currency. This absence was the
direct cause of our single cache/single linked list limitation. The culprit code was

```
/* Cache Module */

#include <stdio.h>
#include "lldef.h"
static int cachesize = 0;
casetsize(size) /* The outside world's access path to cachesize */
int size;
{
  cachesize = size;
}
```

The next routine, `ca_add()`, illustrates the hard coded nature of the cache. This routine added items to the cache. An item was defined as a pointer to the hard coded `itemtype`, a structure defined in `lldef.h`.

```
ca_add(newitem)  /* Add a new item to the cache */
struct itemtype *newitem;
{
/* Add item to list.
   ----------------- */
   if (ll_length() == 0)
      llinit(newitem);
   else
      lladdhead(newitem);

/* Delete an old item if cache is overloaded.
   ----------------------------------------- */
   if (ll_length() > cachesize) {
      lltail();
      lldelete();
   }
}
```

The routine `ca_check()`, shown next, checked the cache for particular items and returned true or false to indicate if the item was located. It also promoted any found items to the head of the linked list, indicating their changed status to ''Most Recently Referenced.'' Not only did this function have the same problem as `ca_add()`, it also had the match function hard wired as `cmpitem()`.

Clients using the original cache module had to provide `cmpitem()`, resolving the reference at linkage time. Programs were thus limited to one instance of `cmpitem()`, and indirectly again to one type of cache. A program could not, for example, maintain a word cache and an I/O cache, because two different versions of `cmpitem()` would be required. `ca_check()` looked like this

```
ca_check(lookfor) /* See if item is in cache */
                  /* Return TRUE or FALSE   */
struct itemtype *lookfor;
{
   struct itemtype lookat;
   cmpitem();

   llhead();
   for (;;) {
      llretrieve (&lookat);
      if (cmpitem(lookfor, &lookat)) {
        lldelete();
        lladdhead(&lookat);
        return (1);
      }
      if (!llnext())
        return (0);
   }
}
```

8.2. GENERALIZING THE CACHE PACKAGE

In this section we will generalize this package to allow clients to determine at run time the number of caches needed, the type of information stored, and the nature of the item comparison. The following summarizes the changes we are about to make

PROGRAM DEFINITION OF CACHE TYPE

- *Before*. Client programmer modified lldef.h to reflect a new linked list, and thereby indirectly modified the cache type. The function cmpitem() was resolved at link time. The linked binaries were different for each application.
- *After*. Header files are never changed. Client programmers change the cache type by calling functions which define the nature of the cache. The function cmpitem() is declared at runtime and changed whenever necessary.

NUMBER OF CACHES USABLE BY ONE PROGRAM

- *Before*. A program had only one cache, and then only if the linked list package was not being used for any other purpose.
- *After*. A program can have an unlimited number of caches, each used for a different purpose, and still have the linked list package available for other purposes as well.

The first change requires taking all information describing a particular cache and packaging into a structure called CACHE. This structure will be application independent. This reorganization is exactly what we saw in Chapters 4 and 5 for the linked list package. A new file, cadef.h, will be created to contain the cache's structural definition.

The file `cadef.h` will allow caches to be defined on an *ad hoc* basis. Two macros, `casetmatch()` and `caitemsize()`, will serve as pass-through functions to the linked list package. Clients will use these macros to define the match function and the size of an item in the cache. These names will shield clients from the underlying linked list implementation. In fact, should this implementation change (not unlikely), these macro definitions would probably be removed and replaced by actual functions.

```
/* cadef.h */
#include "lldef.h"

#define casetmatch llsetmatch   /* define match function */
#define caitemsize llsetsize    /* define size of item in cache */

struct CACHE {
  int cachesize;
  struct LINKLIST clist;
};
```

The global region of the newly organized cache module contains the most significant change. The current cache is no longer hard coded by the linked list package, but is now defined at runtime by whichever cache `ca` addresses.

```
/* Cache Module */

#include <stdio.h>
#include "cadef.h"

static struct CACHE *ca;    /* Pointer to currently active cache. */
```

A new function, `casetcache()`, will be added to allow clients to reset the cache as necessary. Contrary to possible appearances, this function cannot be implemented as a macro pass-through, as was `casetmatch()`, without giving the client access to the critical variable `ca`.

```
casetcache(newcache)
struct CACHE *newcache;
{
  ca = newcache;
  llsetlist (&ca->clist);
}
```

The function `casetsize()` will be purified. Much of its functionality will be moved out to `casetmatch()` and `caitemsize()`.

```
casetsize(size)
int size;
{
  ca->cachesize = size;
}
```

Although `ca_add()` is the most complex function in the module, only two changes are necessary. The parameter `newitem` will be defined as a character pointer instead of a hard-wired `itemtype` structure, and the reference to `cachesize` will be changed to reference the `cachesize` of the current cache.

```
ca_add(newitem)
char *newitem;
{
/* Add item to list.
   ---------------- */
    if (ll_length() == 0)
       llinit(newitem);
    else
       lladdhead(newitem);

/* Delete an old item if cache is overloaded.
   --------------------------------------- */
    if (ll_length() > ca->cachesize) {
       lltail();
       lldelete();
    }
}
```

The function `ca_check()` must have its parameter changed for the same reason as the previous function. We can also simplify it a bit and improve its performance by making use of the more recently defined linked list function `llcheck()`. Lastly, we will add a call to `llretrieve()`. In the specific case of the string cache, the stored item was identical to the requested item, so this call was not needed. The requested item was moved directly to the head of the list. In the general cache case, it is the stored item which must be moved to the head of the list, not the requested item.

```
ca_check(lookfor)
char *lookfor;
{
  llhead();
  if(llcheck(lookfor)) {
    llretrieve(lookfor);
    lldelete();
    lladdhead(lookfor);
    return (1);
  }
  else
    return (0);
}
```

Although we have improved overall functionality, we have also increased client responsibility. The client is now responsible for both declaring and initializing the cache at run time. Actually the client was responsible for initialization, but before it was done at compile time through modifications to `lldef.h`.

The changes needed to improve functionality are minimal, all things considered. This ease in transition is largely a tribute to our initial organization.

8.3. THE I/O PROBLEM

With this fully generalized cache module, we can now return to the problem of writing `get_block()`. A few associated routines are also needed, and they can all go into the module `io.cc`. First we must define an I/O block. Because this definition may be needed in several places, it is placed in the header file `blkdef.h`:

```
/* blkdef.h */
#define BLKSIZE 1024

struct BLKTYPE {
  FILE *file_id;        /* Unique file identifier.                */
  int blk_id;           /* Unique id of this block within the file. */
  char data[BLKSIZE];   /* The information stored in this block.   */
};
```

The module `io.cc` starts by including the necessary header files, the I/O cache, and a scratch block. It also includes a definition for `IO_CACHE_SIZE`, the number of disk blocks to be stored in the cache.

```
/* io.cc */

#include <stdio.h>
#include "cadef.h"
#include "blkdef.h"
#define IO_CACHE_SIZE 3

static struct CACHE ioc;      /* The I/O cache.      */
static struct BLKTYPE iob;    /* An I/O block.       */
```

Described next is a function that will be used to open files whose blocks will be cached. Actually the only real work it performs is to initialize the cache, which is done only with the first call. However it seems easier to tell clients to call this routine for all files rather than confuse the issue.

```
FILE *open_file(file_name)
char *file_name;
{
```

```
FILE *fopen();
static int cmpblocks();
static int firstcall = 1;

if (firstcall) {
  casetcache(&ioc);
  casetmatch(cmpblocks);
  caitemsize(sizeof(struct BLKTYPE));
  casetsize(IO_CACHE_SIZE);
  cazero();
  firstcall = 0;
}
return (fopen(file_name, "rb"));
}
```

Discussed next is a routine that closes files. It is completely unnecessary, and is provided for aesthetic reasons only.

```
close_file (file_id)
FILE *file_id;
{
   fclose (file_id);
}
```

Now we must define the comparison function for the cache package, and indirectly for the linked list package. This routine assumes two blocks are identical if their file IDs and block IDs (or their block offsets) match. It has no reason to check the data portion of the block, because it is used to process client block requests only. The requested block (without data) will be checked against the cache blocks (with data).

```
static int cmpblocks (blk1, blk2)
struct BLKTYPE *blk1, *blk2;
{
   if ((blk1->file_id == blk2->file_id) &&
       (blk1->blk_id == blk2->blk_id))
       return 1;
   else return 0;
}
```

Finally we are ready to establish get_block(), the *raison d'etre* for this entire exercise. This function sets up a temporary work block and then compares it to the blocks stored in the cache. If the requested block is not found, read_block() is called to perform the physical disk read. Finally, regardless of whether the block came from the cache or disk, the requested block is copied into the client's work space.

```
get_block (file_id, blk_id, block)
FILE_*file_id;
int blk_id;
char *block;
{
/* Initialize test block.
   --------------------- */
   casetcache (&ioc);
   iob.file_id = file_id;
   iob.blk_ = blk_id;

/* Get block, either from cache or disk.
   ------------------------------------ */
   if (!ca_check(&iob)) {
     readblock (iob.file_id, iob.blk_id, iob.data);
     ca_add(&iob);
   }
/* Return copy of block to client
   ---------------------------- */
   movmem(iob.data, block, BLKSIZE);
}
```

The function readblock() is obviously highly system dependent. This version uses the
standard routines fseek() and fread() to mimic an actual low level disk read. You can
assume your C library is performing its own disk I/O caching, and the routine as written
may or may not result in an actual disk read.

```
readblock (file_id, blk_id, block)
FILE *file_id;
int blk_id;
char *block;
{
    int offset;
    printf ("readblock called\n");
    offset = BLKSIZE * blk_id;
    fseek (file_id, offset, 0);
    fread (block, BLKSIZE - 1, 1, file_id);
}
```

Now that we have developed an admittedly rudimentary disk I/O cache, let us test it. The
next program, read.cc, opens a file called block.data, queries the user for a block number, and displays the first five characters of the requested block. The program stops when
the user requests a negative block.

```
/* read.cc */

#include <stdio.h>
#include "blkdef.h"
main()
{
/* Set up variables.
   ---------------- */
   FILE *file_id;          /* Unique file identifier. */
   int block_id;           /* Unique block id.        */
   char block[BLKSIZE];    /* A block of data.        */
   int done = 0;           /* Loop controller.        */
   FILE *open_file();

/* Initialize file.
   --------------- */
   file_id = open_file ("block.data");

/* Loop through requested blocks.
   ---------------------------- */
   while (!done) {

/*    Ask for block id and see if done.
      ------------------------------- */
      print ("\nBlock ID: ");
      scanf ("%d", &block_id);
      if (block_id < 0) done = 1;

/*    Retrieve and display block.
      ------------------------- */
      if (!done) {
        get_block (file_id, block_id, block);
        display_block (block);
      }
   }
/* Close file.
   ----------- */
   close_file (file_id);
}
display_block (block)
char *block;
{
  printf("Block: %.5s\n", block);
}
```

As we run this program, pay particular attention to the message identifying calls to readblock(), the low level disk I/O routine. Remember the constant IO_CACHE_SIZE, in io.cc, defined the size of the cache to be three. User input is shown in boldface type.

r read

```
Block ID:  0
readblock called
Block: axxxx

Block ID:  1
readblock called
Block: bxxxx

Block ID:  2
readblock called
Block: cxxxx

Block ID:  1
Block: bxxxx

Block ID:  4
readblock called
Block: exxxx

Block ID:  -1
```

8.4. EXERCISES

1. Explain why readblock() was or wasn't called in each of the block reads shown in the run of read.cc.

2. The I/O cache package as presented can be used only for files that will not be updated. Add another routine called put_block() which will update a block in the cache. This task is not trivial, and will require several changes to the cache module, and possibly changes to the structure BLKTYPE. Pay particular attention to what happens when a block is discarded to make room for a new block. Keep your disk writes to an absolute minimum.

3. In the I/O cache module and lower level routines there are several places where disk blocks are copied from one memory location to another. While much less expensive than a disk read operation, memory copies, especially when they involve such large areas, can be significant factors in I/O performance. Identify every block copy. See which copies can be eliminated with code modifications. Be careful that you do not go too far and accidentally give the client access to your cache buffers. (By the way, why shouldn't you give the client such access?)

4. What changes would allow I/O cache buffers to be shared among many clients, assuming, of course, a multi-process operating system? In other words, if a particular disk block is read by one client, and then requested again by another client, what change would allow us to avoid a disk read? Generalize your solution so that, when necessary, other data structures (such as another linked list) can be shared among users. The implementation of this is operating system dependent. You may use any operating system familiar to you.

CHAPTER 9 **Queues**

By now you should be starting to appreciate reusability. In Chapter 3 we developed a linked list package which, with a few refinements, served as the foundation of every program in this book. We developed a cache package to help search for overused words, and then reused the bulk of the code to create I/O caches. This chapter continues the theme of reusability while introducing a new data structure, a queue. Let us start by considering two programming problems which seem unrelated.

PROBLEM 1

Write a program to search for a specific text string, say *boletes* in a text file. Any line containing the string and the two preceding lines should be printed out. The lines should be printed in the order encountered. A typical input file, and the resulting output is

> *Input File*
> The full mushroom basket of the fall is closed out by a trio of
> beauties: Lepista nebularis, Lepista nuda, and Lepista saeva
> (L. personatum). The first two are found on the borders of mixed
> forests, the third in meadows. If the first attack of winter is not
> too strong, these species may be collected from under the snow. This
> can also happen to the last boletes, and it is curious to find a
> Boletus edulis with a white hat on its cap.

> *Program Output*
> forests, the third in meadows. If the first attack of winter is not
> too strong, these species may be collected from under the snow. This
> can also happen to the last boletes, and it is curious to find a

PROBLEM 2

Construct a hospital emergency room patient management system. As a patient enters the emergency room, a physician assigns a priority ranging from 0 (critical emergency) to 4 (non-emergency). The program accepts the patient's name and priority. When the next physician is available, the program displays the name of the patient who has been waiting the longest at the highest priority. No patients of Priority 1 can be seen as long as priority

100

0 patients are waiting. No Priority 2 patients can be seen until all Priority 1 patients are seen, and so on.

What do these two programming problems have in common? Let us start by first imagining the hospital problem allows only a single priority. Both programs are acquiring and temporarily storing data items. The hospital program stores patient names until the patient is called. The text matcher stores each line of text until the next two lines go by without the desired text string.

Both programs have a similar manner of data retrieval. The hospital retrieves patients in the order they arrive. The text matcher retrieves and prints lines in the order they are encountered.

Differences are also apparent between these two programs. The hospital never discards a patient. All patients are eventually seen. The text matcher discards text lines once they are no longer needed, and under no circumstances ever stores more than three lines at any one time.

If we diagram the data flow for these two programs, visual similarities become apparent. For the hospital program

```
add patient: John
```
```
John
```

```
add patient: Anne
```
```
John — Anne
```

```
add patient: Mary
```
```
John — Anne — Mary
```

```
get patient: (John is retrieved and discarded)
```
```
Anne — Mary
```

```
get patient: (Anne is retrieved and discarded)
```
```
Mary
```

```
get patient: (Mary is retrieved and discarded)
NULL
```

A diagram for the text matcher looks like

L1: The full mushroom basket of the fall is closed out by a trio of
L2: beauties: Lepista nebularis, Lepista nuda, and Lepista saeva

L3: (L. personatum). The first two are found on the borders of mixed
L4: forests, the third in meadows. If the first attack of winter is not
Etc.

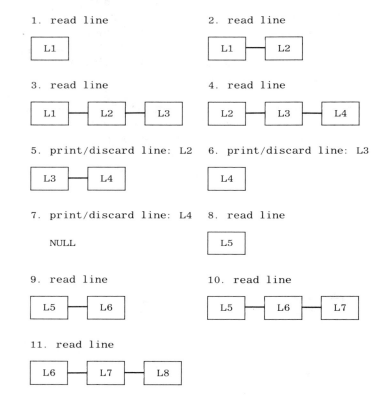

Both programs follow a pattern. The diagrams for each show items added to the right
and removed from the left. Right and left are arbitrary, and may be reversed. The important point is that items are added to one side and removed from the other.

9.1. A QUEUE PACKAGE

The underlying data structure being used by both programs is called a *queue*. A queue is a
storage mechanism in which items are retrieved in the same order as they were entered.
The next item retrieved is the one that resided in storage the longest. This kind of retrieval
is often referred to as FIFO, for First In First Out. Queues conjure up pictures of people on
line for tickets at a theater. The next person off the line is the one who was on line the
longest.

Queues have several alternative implementations (see, for example, Exercise 9.2).

This implementation uses our linked list package. Items are added to the head of the list, and retrieved from the tail, or vice versa. The important point is that items are retrieved from the opposite end as they were added. Placement on the list indicates an item's age.

There are two standard queue primitives, q_push(), for placing items on the queue, and q_pop(), for removing items from the queue. As usual, these primitives and other details of the queue should be neatly packaged, out of the clients' sight.

A fully reusable queue package is significantly easier to implement than even the cache package of the last chapter. A queue can be directly represented as a linked list, unlike a cache which requires a cache structure with an embedded linked list structure.

To keep this implementation transparent we will redefine a queue to be a linked list, and the initializing linked list functions to be initializing queue functions. It is always possible that the underlying implementation of the queue will change and clients must be protected against this possibility. These redefinitions will take place in queuedef.h, which will be included in both the queue module and its client code similar to the use of cadef.h.

```
/* queuedef.h */
#include "lldef.h"

#define qitemsize llsetsize    /* define size of item in queue    */
#define qset llsetlist         /* set current queue               */
#define qlength ll_length      /* Return number of items in queue */

#define QUEUE LINKLIST
```

The queue module proper defines q, a static global pointer to the current queue, used like the analogous current cache pointer, ca, and the current linked list pointer, list.

```
/* queue.cc. */
#include <stdio.h>
#include "queuedef.h"

static struct QUEUE *q;    /* Pointer to currently active queue. */
```

The first operator function has only to check for a first time use.

```
q_push(newitem)
char *newitem;
{
    if (ll_length() == 0)
        llinit(newitem);
    else
        lladdhead(newitem);
}
```

The other operator is even simpler.

```
q_pop(olditem)
char *olditem;
{
    lltail();
    llretrieve(olditem);
    lldelete();
}
```

9.2. TEXT MATCHER

Now that we have a functional queue module, we can solve the first of the problems discussed, the text matcher. As shown in the data flow diagrams, this program will loop
through the text file, read lines and place them in the queue. When a line causes the size of
the queue to exceed three lines, a previous line is removed and discarded. When the most
recent addition is found to contain the requested string, the lines are removed from the
queue and printed until the queue is empty. The program looks like this

```
#include <stdio.h>
#include "queuedef.h"

#define LINES2PRINT 3
main()
{
    static struct QUEUE lineq;
    char line[80], oldline[80];
    int substr();
    int n;

/* Initialize queue.
   ---------------- */
    qset(&lineq);
    qitemsize(sizeof(line));
    while (getline(line) != 0) {

/*    Add item to storage.
      -------------------- */
    q_push(line);
    if (qlength() > LINES2PRINT) {
      q_pop(oldline);
    }
/*    If substring is present, drain queue.
      ------------------------------------- */
    if (substr(line, "boletes")) {
      while (qlength() > 0) {
        q_pop(oldline);
        printf("%s\n", oldline);
      }
    }
  }
}
```

The functions substr() and getline(), if not provided by your C compiler, are easily implemented and not shown.

Most computer systems use queues to coordinate output to line printers. Since only one user can print a file at a time, the system must decide which file is being printed, which files have print requests pending, and in what order pending requests will be handled. The pending requests are usually handled on a first come, first served basis, the essential algorithm of a queue.

9.3. PRIORITY QUEUES

With our queue code in hand, we can return to the hospital problem. Earlier in the chapter we showed how a waiting room of patients could be interpreted as a queue. The next patient waiting to be popped off the queue is the patient who has been waiting the longest, and the one who should next be seen. We simplified the programming problem by imagining it to be a single queue with no associated priorities.

To solve the actual hospital program, we need to bring priorities back into the picture. Recall a patient could have a priority varying from 0 (highest) to 4 (lowest). Within a priority, patients are seen in order of arrival, i.e., using standard queue storage methods.

This type of queue is called a *priority queue*. Priority queues are often implemented as arrays of queues, where the nth element of the array is the queue for priority n. If we were given a queue array called pqueue[], the storage of patients would look like this

Arrival #	Priority	Name
1	2	John
2	3	Anne
3	0	Mary
4	3	Tom
5	0	Les
6	2	Sue
7	1	Stan

Storage

pqueue[0] = Mary, Les
pqueue[1] = Stan
pqueue[2] = John, Sue
pqueue[3] = Anne, Tom
pqueue[4] = NULL

The storage structure may seem daunting at first. After all, we are talking about an array of queues, each of which is really a structure with an embedded linked list. But because of our careful approach to data modularization, this data structure is almost as easy to write as it is to say. The global region of the hospital program looks like this

```
/* Hospital Priority Queue ... hosp.cc */

#include <stdio.h>
#include "queuedef.h"

#define NQUEUES 5
static struct QUEUE pqueue[NQUEUES];
```

Next, some constants are defined for programming style

```
#define NAMELEN 40
#define ADD 1
#define GET 2
#define DONE 3
```

Then we define our main program, which is little more than an overview of the problem

```
main ()
{
   int todo;

/* Initialize.
   ----------- */
   init_pqueue();
   todo = 100;

/* Start looping... ask, do, ask, do, etc.
   ------------------------------------ */
   while (todo != DONE) {
     todo = what_to_do();
     if (todo == ADD) add_patient();
     if (todo == GET) get_patient();
   }
   exit(0);
}
```

The routine init_pqueue() initializes the queue array. One by one, it makes each of the queues current and sets its itemsize.

```
init_pqueue()
{
   int n;
   for (n=0; n<NQUEUES; n++) {
     qset(&pqueue[n]);
     qitemsize(NAMELEN);
   }
   return;
}
```

The function what_to_do() displays a high level menu that asks the user what she wants to do next. A function get_int() is called. It prints a string and waits for the user to enter an integer between the limits of the last two parameters. get_int() is easily written and not shown.

```
what_to_do()
{
    printf(" 1 ... To Add a Patient to the Queue\n");
    printf(" 2 ... To Get an Available Patient\n");
    printf(" 3 ... To Quit Program\n");
    return (get_int("", 1, 3));
}
```

The next function, add_patient(), is called when entering a newly arrived patient. It asks for a priority and a patient name. The priority is used to set the queue currency. Notice that q_push() is called with a string, even though it is expecting a structure pointer. In this case, the structure consists of only a single string, therefore a structure or a string can be used interchangeably. The low level routine getline() is left to the reader's imagination.

```
add_patient()
{
    char patient[NAMELEN];
    int n;
    n = get_int("What Priority?", 0, NQUEUES - 1);
    qset(&pqueue[n]);
    printf ("Patient Name to Add: ");
    getline(patient);
    q_push(patient);
}
```

The function get_patient() is used to tell the doctor which patient should be seen next. It goes through the queues, starting with the highest (pqueue(0)). When a queue is found with at least one patient, the patient is popped off and the function is returned. If no queues have patients, the doctors get to take a coffee break.

```
get_patient()
{
    char patient[NAMELEN];
    int n;

    for (n=0; n<NQUEUES; n++) {
        qset(&pqueue[n]);
        if (qlength() > 0) {
            q_pop(patient);
            printf("Priority: %d Next Patient: %s\n", n, patient);
            return;
        }
    }
    printf ("No patients waiting\n");
}
```

A sample run of this program shows patients added with different priorities. User input is shown in boldface type.

```
   1 ... To Add a Patient to the Queue
   2 ... To Get an Available Patient
   3 ... To Quit Program
   (1 - 3): 1
What Priority? (0 - 4): 2
Patient Name to Add: Andrew

   1 ... To Add a Patient to the Queue
   2 ... To Get an Available Patient
   3 ... To Quit Program
   (1 - 3): 1
What Priority? (0 - 4): 2
Patient Name to Add: John

   1 ... To Add a Patient to the Queue
   2 ... To Get an Available Patient
   3 ... To Quit Program
   (1 - 3): 1
What Priority? (0 - 4): 1
Patient Name to Add: Alice
```

Now we start requesting patients:

```
   1 ... To Add a Patient to the Queue
   2 ... To Get an Available Patient
   3 ... To Quit Program
   (1 - 3): 2
Priority: 1 Next Patient: Alice

   1 ... To Add a Patient to the Queue
   2 ... To Get an Available Patient
   3 ... To Quit Program
   (1 - 3): 2
Priority: 2 Next Patient: Andrew

   1 ... To Add a Patient to the Queue
   2 ... To Get an Available Patient
   3 ... To Quit Program
   (1 - 3): 2
Priority: 2 Next Patient: John
```

Finally, we have used up all of our patients and we quit the program.

```
1 ... To Add a Patient to the Queue
2 ... To Get an Available Patient
3 ... To Quit Program
(1 - 3): 2
No patients waiting

1 ... To Add a Patient to the Queue
2 ... To Get an Available Patient
3 ... To Quit Program
(1 - 3): 3
```

It is worth pausing to consider how nicely package programming simplifies complicated problems. The priority queue definition looked like this

```
static struct QUEUE pqueues[nqueues];
```

It defines, in effect, an array of queues nqueues long. Without package programming, even with no attempt to generalize, we would end up with something like

```
struct queue_type {
  struct queue_type *next;
  char name[100];
};
static struct queue_type *pqueues[n];
```

The modularized package style is very close to the way we, as humans, actually think about this problem. Not only do packages allow us to work with problems that, in Niklaus Wirth's words, are "intellectually manageable," but we end up with reusable, general, tested code to boot.

9.4. OTHER QUEUE APPLICATIONS

Priority queues are often used in Computer Science. Multi-process operating systems in particular use them extensively. Many of the resource management responsibilities of a typical operating system are very similar to the medical resource management responsibilities of the hospital patient manger.

For example, a multi-process operating system must allocate CPU resources equitably among many programs. In Chapter 7 we discussed using linked lists to store information on programs competing for system resources. An active list was made up of the programs waiting to execute—that list was really a queue.

Many operating systems allow priorities to be assigned to programs so that critical programs can be given resource priority over low priority programs. The lowest priority is often assigned to a looping function within the operating system itself. The looping function is responsible for constantly checking to see if any other program is waiting.

An operating system sets up a program information structure for each running program. This structure contains information such as where in memory a program is loaded, the machine state the program expects, and if the program has been temporarily bumped out to disk. Operating systems that have priority mechanisms often store these structures in priority queues. The operating system constantly monitors the priority queue, allowing the program at the head of the highest priority queue to run until the program has either been completed or suspended. A program can be suspended for running through its maximum time limit for consecutive resource usage, or for making a request for a system service, such as a disk I/O operation, which takes time to complete.

When a program is suspended because of a pending request, it goes on a wait list, as we have discussed. When a program is suspended, for example, because its system resource share is exhausted, the program information structure either gets placed back on the end of queue at its current priority or gets demoted to a lower priority queue, depending on the operating system.

Naturally this representation of an operating system is simplified. Nevertheless, the underling data structure, the priority queue, is very similar to the one used by the hospital patient manager.

9.5. EXERCISES

1. Add error checking code to q_pop (), which makes sure a client is not popping from an empty queue.
2. Rewrite the queue module using an array of structures to implement the queue. The reimplementation should have minimal, if any, effect on the client code (the hospital and text matcher, in this case).
3. Our hospital program hard wired the concept of a priority queue. Write a generalized priority queue packet, which allows runtime definition of the information to be stored in the priority queue, and runtime structure resolution. Use the queue packet as a model.
4. The cache module described in Chapter 8 is performance gated on its linked list implementation. To check a cache containing, say, 10 items, we must search, on average, half the cache, or 5 items. A linked list implementation works fine for caches of such small sizes. In Chapter 6 we pointed out that for very large caches, a linked list implementation may be too slow.
   One method for speeding up caches is to use a structure similar to the priority queue, an array of caches. Let us say that we create an array of n caches, similar to the array of queues. Further, let us say that we have a function h () which accepts a cache item, and returns a number randomly but reproducibly distributed between 0 and n. Such a function is called a *hash function*. The algorithm for such a function might be, for the case of I/O caches, the modulus of the blockid and n. In C, this looks like

```
h ()
{
  return (block_id % n)
}
```

With this routine in place, we can implement a hash cache. Take, for example, a hash cache for I/O blocks holding 128 disk blocks. We can set up our array to hold 13 caches of 10 blocks each. To add an I/O block to the cache, first hash its blockid to get a number i between 0 and 12. Set the current cache to be the ith cache in the array, and add the block there. To retrieve an I/O block, follow the same procedure, except check for the block rather than add it.

Implement a reusable hash cache, built on top of the cache module. Keep in mind the application specific nature of hash functions. Although your underlying data structure may seem quite complex, an array of structures containing pointers to linked lists, with careful modularization your code should be straightforward, and only slightly more complicated than the priority queue.

5. In Chapter 8 we saw how disk I/O can be significantly reduced by using a disk block cache. The routine get_block() initiated low level I/O only when the necessary block was not in the cache. Low level I/O was the responsibility of readblock(), which accepted as parameters the requested fileid and blockid. If, despite our I/O cache, a large number of disk reads are being done, what can we do to make them as efficient as possible?

Most operating systems treat a disk as if it were composed of physical areas, each holding disk blocks. Usually a relationship exists between the time it takes to read two blocks, and how widely apart their areas are. For example, if we want to read Block x, which lies in Area 1, and Block y, the total read time will be less if Block y also lives in Area 1: the time will be longer if Block y lives in Area 2: and even longer if Block y lives in Area 3, and so on. This time factor occurs because moving from area to area requires physical movement of the disk read heads. Usually the fastest way to read a collection of disk blocks is not to read them in the order they are requested, but in area order. In other words, the I/O time can be significantly reduced by first reading all requested blocks in Area 1, then all requested blocks in Area 2, etc. Within an area, order is less important, so we might as well read blocks in the order they are requested. Write a function setup_read() to replace the call to read_block() in the Chapter 8 I/O code. This function will add your disk read request to a data structure designed to expedite disk reads along these lines. Assume you have access to a function get_area(), which takes a file_id and block_id and returns an area between 1 and 100. Assume also that your responsibility ends when the read request is added to the "read_request" structure you design, and actual low level disk I/O is coordinated by a separate process.

CHAPTER 10 **Stacks**

The previous chapter showed another example of how the same data manipulation code could be made to serve two masters, a text scanner and a hospital patient information manager. The package consisted of generalized data structures and application independent primitives.

This chapter shows two more examples of programming problems, which, though quite different, share underlying structures. We will also see another advantage of package programming—how one package can be copied, modified slightly, and turned into a different package with new primitives and completely different data characteristics. But first, let us look at the problems.

10.1. MEMORY ALLOCATION

By now you should be familiar with the standard C functions `malloc()` and `free()`. We will now write similar, but easier to use functions. A program is expected to call `free()` once for every call made to `malloc()`. This call fulfills its responsibility to return memory to the dynamic memory pool once the memory is no longer needed. We will write three functions with these characteristics:

- get_mem()–This procedure works exactly like `malloc()`. It accepts one parameter, the number of memory bytes needed, and returns a pointer to a memory block.
- mark_stack()—This procedure, with no parameters, marks a moment in time.
- rel_mem()—This procedure releases all memory allocated with get_mem() since the last call to mark_stack().

These three functions allow a user to mark a moment of time in the stack, allocate several chunks of memory, and then, with one call to rel_mem(), release all memory chunks allocated since the time was marked. And because mark_stack() can be called several times, we can release memory back to one previous mark, allocate more memory, then de-allocate even more. The following program shows the use of these three functions:

```
main()
{
    char *p1, *p2, *p3, *p4, *p5, *p6, *p7, *p8;
    char *get_mem();
    mark_stack();
    p1 = get_mem(10);
    p2 = get_mem(10);
    p3 = get_mem(10);
    p4 = get_mem(10);
    mark_stack();
    p5 = get_mem(10);
    p6 = get_mem(10);
    p7 = get_mem(10);
    p8 = get_mem(10);
    rel_mem();
    rel_mem();
}
```

If we diagram what is occurring in this program, we see the following sequence. First, `mark_stack()` is called:

MARK

Then four calls are made to `mem_get()`:

MARK-p1-p2-p3-p4

Then another call is made to `mark_stack()`, followed by four calls to `get_mem()`:

MARK-p1-p2-p3-p4-MARK-p5-p6-p7-p8

The next call is made to `rel_mem()` and it releases the four memory chunks allocated since the last `mark_stack()`. These are the memory blocks whose addresses are p8, p7, p6, and p5. Our data storage now looks like

MARK-p1-p2-p3-p4

The next `rel_mem()` frees all data to the last mark, which is everything left.

The storage mechanism returns items to us in the reverse order as they were stored. So, the last item stored is the next item returned. This order contrasts with the data structures of Chapter 9, where data items were retrieved in the same order as they were stored. Before we delve too deeply into this new data structure, let us consider a different problem.

10.2. DATABASE RECORD INSERT

The second problem to consider here is to construct the record entry part of a database system. A user is presented with the current state of a record, and is allowed to make changes. When the user is satisfied with the state of the record, the record is stored. The interesting part of this action is that the user must also be allowed to undo changes. When the undo option is chosen, the system restores the record to its state before the last modification. If necessary, every modification can be undone, right up to the original state of the record.

Although this problem seems quite different from the memory manager problem, they do share one common need—both require the ability to store and retrieve some type of item, and the order of retrieval needs to be the reverse of storage, with the next item retrieved being the item most recently stored.

This type of storage is often ambiguously referred to as LIFO, for Last In, First Out. Such storage is called a *stack*. A stack is often pictured as being like a stack of dishes. When you take a plate off a stack, the plate you remove is the one you most recently added.

10.3. A STACK PACKAGE

A stack is conceptually the exact opposite of a queue. A queue returns items in the same order as they were stored. A stack returns items in the reverse order as they were stored. Is there any hope of modifying our queue package to make it work as a stack?

Actually just one small difference lies between our queue and stack modules. Both can use a linked list to store items. Both can add items to the head of a list. However a stack returns items from the head, whereas a queue returns items from the tail. At this point you may want to study the queue primitives in Chapter 9, and determine the changes you think will be necessary.

As you examine the following stack module, notice there is only one minor logic change from the queue module. Other than that change, only the names of identifiers have been changed to reflect the stack's functionality.

The header file, stackdef.h contains the definition of the stack type. Like the queue, the stack can be directly represented as a linked list.

```
/* stackdef.h */
#include "lldef.h"

#define stitemsize llsetsize   /* define size of item in stack */
#define stset llsetlist        /* set current stack            */
#define stlength ll_length

#define STACK LINKLIST
```

The module for the stack primitives, stack.cc starts with the currency pointer, st, whose purpose you should now know.

```
/* Stack Module: stack.cc */

#include <stdio.h>
#include "stackdef.h"

static struct STACK *st;    /* Pointer to currently active stack. */
```

The function st_push() is identical to the analogous queue routine.

```
st_push(newitem)
char *newitem;
{
    if (ll_length() == 0)
        llinit(newitem);
    else
        lladdhead(newitem);
}
```

The function st_pop() contains the only substantial change from the similar queue function. We will leave the change to the reader to detect.

```
st_pop(olditem)
char *olditem;
{
    llretrieve(olditem);
    lldelete();
}
```

10.4. MEMORY ALLOCATION IMPLEMENTATION

This memory allocation problem may seem superficially similar to the problem in Chapter 7, which also dealt with memory allocation. The module in Chapter 7 was a garbage collector, responsible for efficient utilization of memory. The module in this chapter is really designed to simplify allocation, and more specifically, the de-allocation of memory. In fact, even though both modules work with memory management, the two modules have very little in common. They do not use the same data primitives. They do not even store similar information.

The Garbage Collector was required to store the address of a memory pointer so that the pointer itself could be updated when the memory was reshuffled. The Memory Allocator does not rearrange memory, and needs only to store the addresses of the memory blocks that will later be passed through to free().

The algorithms for the three memory allocation functions are straightforward. Assume that an item can either be a memory address or a MARK. The mark_stack() pushes a MARK onto the stack. The function get_mem() calls malloc() to allocate some memory. It then pushes the address onto the stack and returns the address. Finally, the function rel_mem() loops until finding a MARK, pops items off and frees their addresses.

In the global region of the memory allocation module, the stack is declared, and a pnt_type structure is declared containing either addresses or marks. This structure is the application specific information that moves on and off the stack.

```
#include "stackdef.h"

static struct STACK memstk;   /* Stack of memory pointers. */

struct pnt_type {
    int type;       /* Either IS_MARK or IS_PNT.    */
    char *pnt;      /* Address of allocated memory.  */
};

#define IS_MARK 0  /* Type for stack marker.   */
#define IS_PNT  1  /* Type for pointer.            */

static struct pnt_type pointer;
```

The function mark_stack() sets the stack currency, initializes the stack, and pushes a MARK.

```
mark_stack()
{
    static int first = 1;

/* Initialize stack if first time through.
   -------------------------------------- */
    stset(&memstk);
    if (first) {
        stitemsize(sizeof(struct pnt_type));
        first = 0;
    }
/* Mark the stack.
   --------------- */
    pointer.type = IS_MARK;
    st_push(&pointer);
}
```

Next, get_mem() calls malloc() to allocate a chunk of memory, and pushes (and returns) the memory address. This function assumes set_mark() was the first routine called, and therefore does not perform initialization.

```
char *get_mem(nbytes)
int nbytes;            /* Number of bytes requested. */
{
    char *malloc();

    stset(&memstk);
    pointer.type = IS_PNT;
    pointer.pnt = malloc(nbytes);
    st_push(&pointer);
    return (pointer.pnt);
}
```

Finally, `rel_mem()` pops memory off the stack and releases it.

```
rel_mem()
{
    stset(&memstk);
    st_pop(&pointer);
    while (pointer.type == IS_PNT) {
        free(pointer.pnt);
        st_pop(&pointer);
    }
}
```

10.5. DATABASE RECOVERY

The code required to deal with database data entry and recovery is more complicated, primarily because the user is a human. Humans are always much more difficult to interact with than other functions. A pseudocode solution to the data entry problem looks like this

```
while(!done) {
    display record;
    ask which field to change;
    if (change desired) {
        push old value;
        get new value;
    }
    if (undo desired) {
        pop old value;
    }
    see if we are done;
}
```

A database record will be defined as an array of field structures. Each field structure will contain a field number, a prompt (to be displayed to the user), and a value. A typical field could contain these structure items:

```
field number: 1
      prompt: Last Name
       value: Hancock
```

A structure of this type will contain information for the stack. The global region of the database program will contain this field structure definition and some constants:

```
/* dbstack.cc */

#include <stdio.h>
#include "stackdef.h"
struct fldtype {
  int fldno;
  char prompt [80];
  char value [80];
};
#define NFIELDS  3   /* Number of fields in record. */
#define FINISHED -1
#define UNDO -2
```

The definition of a database record, the array db_rec, and the stack definition comes early in the main program. The rest of the main program is a translation of the pseudocode. Actually, as in most cases, once the underlying data structures are worked out, the remaining work is automatic, almost mechanical.

```
main()
{
/* Declarations
   ------------ */
   struct fldtype db_rec[NFIELDS];
   struct fldtype field;
   int done, nxtfld;
   static struct STACK dbstk;   /* Stack of old field values. */

/* Initialize.
   ----------- */
   done = 0;
   init_rec(db_rec);
   stset(&dbstk);
   stitemsize(sizeof(struct fldtype));

/* Start looping.
   -------------- */
   while(!done) {

/*   Display record and see if changes are needed.
     --------------------------------------------- */
     disp_rec(db_rec);
     nxtfld = wh_fld();
```

```
/*    If (change desired)
      ------------------ */
      if (nxtfld >= 0) {

/*    Store current field in case they change their mind.
      -------------------------------------------------- */
      st_push(&db_rec[nxtfld]);

/*    Now get a new value.
      ------------------- */
      get_fld(&db_rec[nxtfld]);
    }
/*    If (undo desired) Undo the last change.
      ------------------------------------- */
      if (nxtfld == UNDO) {
        st_pop(&field);
        memcpy(&db_rec[field.fldno], &field, sizeof(struct fldtype));
      }
/*    See if we are done.
      ------------------ */
      if (nxtfld == FINISHED) done = 1;
    }
}
```

The function init_rec() fills a database record with its three initial fields and their values. For example, first name, last name, and city/state, would be filled with the values John, Hancock, and Boston, MA.

```
init_rec(db_rec)
struct fldtype db_rec[];
{
   int n;
   static char *init_prompt [] =
   {
     "First Name",
     "Last Name",
     "City, State"
   };
   static char *init_value [] =
   {
     "John",
     "Hancock",
     "Boston, MA,"
   };
   for (n=0; n < NFIELDS; n++) {
     db_rec[n].fldno = n;
     strcpy(db_rec[n].prompt, init_prompt[n]);
     strcpy(db_rec[n].value, init_value[n]);
   }
}
```

The next function displays a database record.

```
disp_rec(db_rec)
struct fldtype db_rec[];
{
    int n;
    for (n=0; n < NFIELDS; n++)
      printf ("%d. %25s: %s\n",
      db_rec[n].fldno, db_rec[n].prompt, db_rec[n].value);
}
```

The next function asks for a field number to change. This procedure is followed by a function that asks for a new field value.

```
wh_fld()
{
    int answer = -100;

    printf
    ("Enter field number, -1 to store, or -2 to undo last change ");
    while (answer < UNDO || answer >= NFIELDS)
      scanf ("%d", &answer);
    return answer;
}
get_fld(fld)
struct fldtype *fld;
{
    printf ("New value: ");
    scanf ("%s", fld->value);
}
```

Now we can look at a typical program run. The fields are numbered 0 through 2. If the user enters a field number, he is prompted for a new value for that field. If he enters –1, the record is stored. If he enters –2, the system undoes the last change, and displays the record as it was before the last field modification. The example shows user input in bold-face type.

```
0.               First Name: John
1.                Last Name: Hancock
2.               City/State: Boston, MA.

Enter field number, -1 to store, or -2 to undo last change: 0
New value: Henry
```

```
0.                   First Name:  Henry
1.                    Last Name:  Hancock
2.                   City/State:  Boston, MA.
```

Enter field number, -1 to store, or -2 to undo last change: **0**
New value: **Howard**

```
0.                   First Name:  Howard
1.                    Last Name:  Hancock
2.                   City/State:  Boston, MA.
```

Enter field number, -1 to store, or -2 to undo last change: **-2**

```
0.                   First Name:  Henry
1.                    Last Name:  Hancock
2.                   City/State:  Boston, MA.
```

Enter field number, -1 to store, or -2 to undo last change: **-2**

```
0.                   First Name:  John
1.                    Last Name:  Hancock
2.                   City/State:  Boston, MA.
```

Enter field number, -1 to store, or -2 to undo last change: **-1**

Stacks are found in diverse areas such as compilers, artificial intelligence, and operating systems. Many computers have stack instructions implemented within their hardware. Stacks are often part of the processing of function calls, where they may be associated with parameter passing, allocation of space for automatic variables, and the transfer of control at the start and end of invocation. In fact, most modern languages are dependent on the use of stacks to support recursion.

10.6. EXERCISES

1. The stack packet in this chapter used a linked list implementation. Stacks can also be implemented with arrays. A variable called the stack index points to the last array element. The primitive push() is implemented by incrementing the stack index and copying to the last array element. The primitive push() is implemented by decrementing the index and copying from the last array element. The stack index also shows how many elements are on a stack at any given time.

    The array implementation is a little more difficult to generalize than the linked list implementation, partially because it has to be built from scratch. However there are some situations when it is preferred. These situations include

- If you know the maximum size of the stack/queue. Especially if the maximum and the average are close, you do not have to waste memory allocating for the worst case.
- If speed is critical, in which case you should also consider implementing the primitives as macro definitions.
- If simple values are being passed and "copying" can be done with an arithmetic assignment statement.

The Memory Allocator described in this chapter is a possible candidate for an array-stack. One contra-indication in this case is the lack of a simple value. We could solve this problem by using a NULL pointer to indicate a mark.

Rewrite the memory allocator to use an array implementation for the stack. Make as few changes to the memory allocation module as possible. Instead, write a new stack module. Assume speed is important and replace function calls by macros wherever possible. Use a separate header file to define these macros (refer to 11_xpnd.h in Chapter 6).

2. Write a program to conduct interviews. This program should interactively ask the following questions (user input is shown in boldface type):

```
What is your name? Flora
Flora, what is your age? 35
What is your sex? Enter M for male, F for female: f
What is your marital status, Please type
   1 If you are currently married.
   2 If you were previously married, but not currently married.
   3 If you have never been married.
Marital Status: 1
What is your profession? Mycologist
What is your annual income? 45,000
```

Only if a person is currently married, ask the following questions about the spouse, changing the sex as appropriate:

```
What is your husband's name? Tom
What is Tom's profession? Firefighter
What is his annual income? 38,000
```

If a person is either currently or previously married, ask the following questions about the children. Notice that this program assumes that only people who are married can have children. The program is a little naive regarding this point.

```
Flora, How many children do you have? 2
```

For each child, ask

```
What is your first child's name? Mary
What is Mary's sex? Enter M for male, F for female: f
How old is she? 7
Is she in school? (Y for yes, N for no): y
```

if yes, then

What grade? **4**

if no, then

What is her profession? **teacher**
What is her annual income? **23,000**

This program should ask questions intelligently. For example, if a child is in school, the program should not ask for the child's profession.

The program should allow answers to be changed. At any time during the program the interviewee should be able to type $ instead of the current question, indicating the interviewee has reconsidered a previous question and wants to change the answer. The program should then display all previous questions and answers, ask which answer she wants to change, allow the answer to be changed, and then pick up where it left off.

At the end of the interviewing session, your program should print out the results, ready to be analyzed by a statistician.

Think about these problems before starting work:
- How are you going to control the flow of questions?
- How are you going to return to previous questions?
- How are you going to store answers?
- What will you do when the interviewee changes an answer (such as "Are you married?") that changes the course of the interview.

Develop a structure to contain the information needed to ask a particular question. You have several possibilities here. You could write separate functions for each question, and then include in the question structure the address of the next function to be called. You could try to write a generic question-asking function, and then include more information in the structure to individualize the question at run time.

Use a question stack to control the order of questions. As soon as you are sure a question needs to be asked, push the appropriate question structure onto the stack. The pseudocode for this program looks something like this

```
initialize question stack
while (stack is not empty) {
  pop question off
  ask question
  if (user types $) {
     push question back on
     see what they want to change
     push that question on stack
  }
}
```

This program structure allows you to interrupt the flow if the user decides to change a previous answer. You determine which question they want to change and push its structure onto the stack. This interruption will have no effect on the later flow.

   Your program can control the flow of questions by popping a question off the stack and then calling the appropriate function. Once in a function, you can pop an element off to tell what type and how many parameters follow, and then pop the parameters off one by one.

   Regardless of whether you choose to write specific or generic question functions, you will probably need to pass information to your function(s). Different amounts and types of information may be necessary for different questions. Define your stack elements to be either function addresses, or parameters to a function. This definition is similar to how compilers use stacks to set up parameter passing.

   The design of the storage structures that will represent the answers is left to you. Consider using one or more of the packages presented in previous chapters.

CHAPTER 11 **Recursives**

11.1. RECURSIVES

We have now developed reusable data manipulation packages for caches, queues and stacks, all using the linked list packages. Other building blocks could have been used, but the linked list was readily available.

All of these structures were implemented so that they could be applied to a variety of client code problems. We eliminated restrictions concerning both the number of structures and internal package conflicts.

Another characteristic shared by these packages is the essentially non-recursive nature of their algorithms. This chapter examines data structures manipulated by recursive algorithms. A recursive algorithm is, loosely speaking, one that is defined in terms of itself. All recursive algorithms have two important features in common. First, they have at least one condition within which they need to solve their own algorithms with different input. This condition is called the *recursive condition*. Second, they have at least one condition within which a result can be computed without recourse to recursion. This condition is called the *terminal condition*.

Actually, the linked list structure we used could have been defined recursively. It was not however for reasons of efficiency. For example, the algorithm we used for searching was non-recursive, or iterative, and looked like this

```
search_list()
{
    until (end of list) {
      get next link;
      if (this link matches) return TRUE;
      else {
        get next link;
        if (there are no more links) return FALSE;
      }
    }
}
```

The recursive version of this algorithm would look like this

```
search_list()
{
  if (this link matches) return TRUE;
  if (there are no more links) return FALSE;
  else {
    set current link to next link;
    return (search_list());
  }
}
```

The recursive version of search_list() depends on the recursive nature of the data structure. Every link in the linked list is either a terminal link or the start of a new linked list. If a desired item is not in the current link, then we must determine which of the structure types we are dealing with. If the link is a terminal link, we are finished; the answer is not found. If the link is the start of another list, then we return the result of applying the algorithm to the remainder of the list.

As expected, both recursive and terminal conditions are present in this version of search_list(). The terminal condition occurs when either the item we are searching for is in the current link, or we have no more links. The recursive condition occurs when we have not yet found what we are searching for and we are not yet at the end of the list.

It is important to understand how variable storage is treated for recursive functions. Although storage is handled no differently for recursive functions, the storage implications are important. Consider a recursive algorithm that calculates factorial numbers, albeit inefficiently. The factorial of n, written n! is defined as

$$n! = n-1 * n-2 * n-3 * \ldots * 1$$

For example

$$5! = 5 * 4 * 3 * 2 * 1 = 120$$

Although the non-recursive (iterative) solution, using a for loop, is most efficient, a recursive solution serves well to illustrate how variable storage is treated. It is also a good example of recursion in general. A recursive function for factorial looks like this

```
fact(n)
int n;
{
  if (n == 1) return 1;
  else return n * fact(n-1);
}
```

This function can be used like this

```
#include <stdio.h>
main ()
{
  int n = 3;
  print("Factorial of %d is %d\n", n, fact(n));
}
```

```
Output:
Factorial of 3 is 6
```

The terminal condition for this function occurs when the function is called to solve the factorial of 1. The recursive condition occurs when the function is called with anything else. To dissect this function, we must blow it apart and add some trace statements:

```
fact (n)
int n;
{
  static int call_number = 0;
  int result, next, param;
  call_number++;
  param = n;
  printf ("Starting fact ... call number: %d n: %d\n",
  call_number, param);
  if (param == 1) {
    printf ("No recursion necessary\n");
    result = 1;
  }
  else {
    next = param - 1;
    printf ("About to recurse for n:%d\n", next);
    result = fact(next);
    printf ("fact returned: %d\n", result);
    result = param * result;
  }
  printf ("Returning: %d\n", result);
  return result;
}
```

The output from this modified function with lines numbered for later reference looks like this

```
1.   Starting fact ... call number: 1 n: 3
2.   About to recurse for n:2
3.   Starting fact ... call number: 2 n: 2
4.   About to recurse for n:1
5.   Starting fact ... call number: 3 n: 1
6.   No recursion necessary
```

```
7.  Returning: 1
8.  fact returned: 1
9.  Returning: 2
10. fact returned: 2
11. Returning: 6
```

Each of these lines gives us clues about how the recursion works. Correspond the number labels from the function output to the following list:

1. The function is called to solve fact(3).

2. We are in the recursive condition, so we need to recursively calculate fact(2).

3. The function is called a second time *by itself* to solve fact(2). The static variable call_number shows the same memory location as the call_number in the initial invocation. Also the increment from the first invocation is seen here.

4. We are in the recursive condition again, so we need to recursively calculate fact(1). Again we see previous modifications to the static call_number carried forward in this recursive call.

5. The function is called for the third time, again by itself, to solve fact(1).

6. We are asked to solve fact(1), which is a terminal condition, and no recursion is necessary.

7. We return 1, the factorial of 1.

8. We now return to the second call of fact(), and have all the information necessary to calculate fact(2), which is 2 * 1. The automatic variable param was not destroyed by the recursion. If it had been, this algorithm would not work. We can conclude that automatic variables, unlike static variables, are re-allocated with each invocation, and therefore are protected against being overwritten. The variable param of invocation 1 is pointing at a different memory location than the params of invocations 2 and 3.

9. We return 2, the factorial of 2.

10. We now return to the first call of fact(), and have the necessary information to calculate fact(3), which is 3 * 2.

11. We return for the last time, now to the program that called us, with the fact() result that it requested.

11.2. BINARY TREES

With recursion under our belts, let us look at a class of data structures which, unlike linked lists, cannot easily be manipulated with iterative algorithms. These structures fall in a general class called *trees*. There are many types of trees: AVL Trees (named for Adel'son-Vel'skiĭ and Landis), Tries, and B Trees, and others. This chapter looks at one representative of the genus, the Binary Tree, because it is typical of the programming problems you will encounter when creating reusable packages for this class of structures. The other types of trees are covered in other books.

First, let us see exactly what a binary tree is. It is similar to a linked list, but has one important difference. A linked list has at most one possibility for the next link; binary trees have at most two. Aside from this difference these two data structures are surprisingly similar.

This seemingly insignificant difference actually opens up some rich programming possibilities. The kinds of algorithms associated with binary trees are sometimes described as *divide and conquer*, because each time you choose one of the two exit points from a link, you eliminate half of the remaining links.

Think of a link, or a node, as it is usually referred to in tree discussions, as being analogous to a room with one entrance and two exits. Each of the two exit doors leads to a similar room. A locked exit means that there are no further rooms in that direction. Suppose further that a room can contain some kind of item.

For example, let us say that each room contains a blackboard on which can be written a word. Let us also assume that the creator of this maze used these rules: the left exit door, if unlocked, leads to a room whose word is alphabetically less than or equal to the word in the current room; the right exit door, if unlocked, leads to a room with a word alphabetically larger.

If this maze contained 60,000 rooms, how many would we have to go through to find a particular word, say *mushroom*? A typical scenario might look like this

1. We enter the first room which contains *landlubber*. Because our word is alphabetically bigger, we take the right exit. The rules tell us we have eliminated all of the rooms containing words less than *landlubber*.

2. The right exit takes us to a room containing the word *spineless*. Because *mushroom* is alphabetically smaller than *spineless*, we take the left exit.

3. We enter the *preposterous* room, and take the left exit.

4. We enter the *nerve-wracking* room, and take the left exit.

5. We enter the *meaningless* room, and this time exit right.

6. We enter the *miserable* room, and exit right.

7. We enter the *mushroom* room, and we are finished.

Unfortunately other scenarios exist as well. Consider this sequence, which also follows the maze rules:

1. We enter the *absurd* room, and exit right.

2. We enter the *accursed* room, and exit right.

3. We enter the *adolescent* room, and exit right.

4. We enter the *alarming* room, and exit right.

5. We enter the *alienated* room, and exit right.

6. We enter the *allusive* room, and exit right.

7. We enter the *amanita* room, and exit right.
Etc.

In the first scenario, we go through 7 rooms to find the one word out of 60,000 we are looking for. Even if we had needed to continue our search a little longer, we had a strong sense of continuing progress. In the second scenario, we also go through 7 rooms, but seem to make little, if any, progress. What is the difference?

In the first scenario, the maze appears evenly distributed. In any given room, there is about as much of the maze to our right as to our left. In the second scenario, the maze appears heavily biased toward the right. In the first scenario, we are eliminating roughly half of all remaining words with each exit choice. In the second scenario, we are eliminating only a very small percentage, unless by chance the word we are looking for is in the very early part of the alphabet.

An unbiased tree, usually referred to as a *balanced* tree, is one in which each room has about as much of the remaining maze to the right as to the left. How long will it take to find our room, in an unbiased maze? Following from the definition, upon exiting the first room, we eliminate half of the 60,000 rooms, or 30,000. With the second exit, we eliminate half of the remaining 30,000 or 15,000. With the third exit, we are down to 7,500, the fourth, 3,750, and so on until by the sixteenth choice, there are only two possible rooms left, the one on the left and the one on the right. If the maze is really unbiased, this case is the worst possible.

A binary tree is called a recursive data structure because several of the binary tree primitives are most easily defined recursively. One such primitive is tree traversal, which takes us through the tree applying a function to each node. If, say, the function is printing, tree traversal may consist of displaying the contents of each room in alphabetical order. The recursive algorithm for such a traversal is

```
traverse(tree)
{
  if (left door is unlocked)
     traverse(tree starting with left door)
  display this room
  if (right door is unlocked)
     traverse(tree starting with right door)
}
```

In this algorithm, two conditions are recursive (the left or right door is unlocked) and one condition is terminal (both doors are locked). We can see how this algorithm works by looking at traversal of this representative balanced tree:

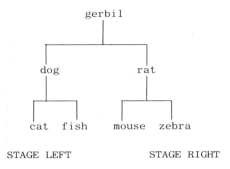

A traversal trace shows

- We start traversal in the gerbil room. The left door is unlocked, so we recursively start traversal through the left door, the dog room.
- Again the left door is unlocked, so we recursively start traversal in the cat room.
- The left door is locked, so we display cat, and return to the caller, which is traversal in the dog room.
- We have now completed the first part of traversal in the dog room, and proceed to the second part, which is to display the contents of this room, dog.
- We are now ready for the third part of traversal in the dog room, which is to check the right door, and recursively traverse through the fish room.
- Both doors are locked in the fish room, so we display the contents, fish, and return to the caller, traversal in the dog room.
- We have now completed the third and final part of traversal in the dog room, and return to our caller, traversal in the gerbil room.
- We have now completed the first part of traversal in the gerbil room, and proceed to the second part, display gerbil.
- The following words have at this point been displayed

```
cat dog fish gerbil
```

- Now we start displaying the words bigger than gerbil. The reader is invited to complete the algorithm.

Another recursive binary tree primitive is `add()`, the primitive used to add items to the appropriate locations in the tree. The algorithm for adding a new item looks like this

```
add(item)
{
  If (item is less than or equal to item in this room)
     nextdoor = left door;
  Else
     nextdoor = right door;
  If (nextdoor is locked)
     unlock nextdoor and add item to next room;
  Else ;
     enter nextdoor;
     add(item);
  }
}
```

Let us see how this algorithm works when a kangaroo is added to the animal tree:

- We enter the gerbil room. Kangaroo is bigger than gerbil, so the exit is stage right.
- The next door is unlocked, so we go through it to the rat room.
- We solve the same algorithm in the rat room.
- Kangaroo is less than rat, so the next exit is stage left.
- The next door is unlocked, so we go through to the mouse room, and start the algorithm again.
- Kangaroo is less than mouse, so the next exit is stage left.
- Stage left is locked. We unlock the door, toss in the kangaroo, and we are finished.

The tree now looks like this

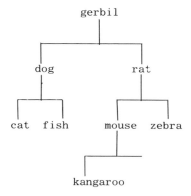

Before we look at the code required for a reusable, recyclable, binary tree package, let us determine which features of such a tree are application specific, and which are general.

First, the item being stored in a room is clearly application specific, and can be managed much like the application specific items of our linked list package.

Second, the nature of an item comparison is application specific. Items are constantly compared during the addition process. Comparison depends on the items, the operation, and the application. This feature also is similar to the situation with the linked list package.

Third, the function applied at each node during traversal depends on both the application and the nature of the items stored. In the animal room traversal we printed the room contents at each node. For other applications we might print part of the item contents, take a count, or perform some other function.

Finally, we can even consider the order of traversal as application specific. To print the tree in ascending order, we applied the print function to the left sub-tree, then to its node, and finally to the right sub-tree. This pattern is a left, node, right traversal. To print the tree in descending order, the function would be applied to the right sub-tree, then to its node, and finally to the left sub-tree. This pattern is a right, node, left traversal.

11.3. BINARY TREE IMPLEMENTATION

The code required to create an application independent binary tree package starts with a btdef.h file, analogous to the lldef.h file for linked lists. The file assigns names to the three possible traversal directions.

```
/* btdef.h */

#define LNR 1 /* Left, Node, Right */
#define RNL 2 /* Right, Node, Left */
#define LRN 3 /* Left, Right, Node */
```

Next we must define a node, or what we have allegorically called a room. As described, the definition contains two possible exits and a pointer to the application specific structure, the item that lives in the room. This definition is similar to the generic definition of a link within a linked list.

```
struct btnode_type {
    struct btnode_type *left;
    struct btnode_type *right;
    char *item;
};
```

Now we have a structure that contains both the runtime and application specific information used by the tree as a whole. This structure serves the same function for binary trees as the structure LINKLIST served for linked lists.

```
struct BINARYTREE {
    struct btnode_type *root;        /* Root of tree.          */
    struct btnode_type *current_node; /* Current node.         */
    int itemlength;                  /* Size of item in node.  */
    int trav_direction;              /* Direction of traversal. */
    int (*less)();                   /* Two functions to com-  */
    int (*eq)();                     /* pare items.            */
};
/* End of btdef.h */
```

With this header file completed, we can start on the binary tree module itself. All functions can be placed in the file bt.cc, enabling effective use of the global variable cbt, which points to the current binary tree of interest. This variable serves the same function as list in the linked list module. Again, like the linked list module, we see a simplified macro definition for movmem(), in the early sections of the module.

```
/* bt.cc */

#include <stdio.h>
#include "btdef.h"

static struct BINARYTREE *cbt;  /* Current BT */

/* Use this macro as moveitem(from, to) */
#define moveitem(A,B) movmem(A,B,cbt->itemlength)
```

The first routine in the module is used by client code to set tree currency, just as llsetlist() was used to set linked list currency.

```
bt_settree(newtree)
struct BINARYTREE *newtree;
{
    cbt = newtree;
}
```

The next routine allocates space for a new node. It is only used internally, and so it is declared static. The function is similar to the linked list routine llcrlink().

```
static struct btnode_type *create_node()
{
    char *malloc();
    struct btnode_type *newnode;

    newnode = (struct btnode_type *)malloc(sizeof(struct btnode_typ e));
    newnode->item = malloc(cbt->itemlength);
    newnode->left = NULL;
    newnode->right = NULL;
    return newnode;
}
```

The function `bt_init()` is used by clients to initialize a binary tree for the first time. It has a similar, but not identical purpose to the linked list function `llinit()`.

```
bt_init(btless,bteq, btdirect, btsize)
int (*btless)();      /* Function to see if item 1 less than item 2. */
int (*bteq)();        /* Function to see if item 1 equal to item 2.  */
int btdirect;         /* Set the traversal direction. */
int btsize;           /* Size of an item in this tree. */
{
    cbt->root = NULL;
    cbt->current_node = NULL;
    cbt->less = btless;
    cbt->eq = bteq;
    cbt->trav_direction = btdirect;
    cbt->itemlength = btsize;
}
```

The function `init_tree()` is another function used only internally. It adds a new node to an *empty* tree. Once a first node has been added, the tree by definition has exactly one node. Both the tree root and current node pointer are set to this node.

This function will be called when a binary tree module realizes that it is being asked to add a node to an empty tree. This function is dependent on a prior call to `bt_init()`.

```
static init_tree(item)
char *item;
{
    struct btnode_type *newnode;
    static struct btnode_type *create_node();

    newnode = create_node();
    moveitem(item, newnode->item);
    cbt->current_node = cbt->root = newnode;
    return;
}
```

The next function, `bt_setroot()`, sets the current node pointer to the tree root. Client code may need to call this function, so it is allowed to default to external.

```
bt_setroot()
{
    cbt->current_node = cbt->root;
}
```

The next function, `bt_examine()`, is a user gate to the item stored in the current node. It allows clients to retrieve the address of an item without having to be aware of either the

storage mechanism or how the binary tree is constructed. In other words, it returns the
address of an item.

```
char *bt_examine()
{
    return cbt->current_node->item;
}
```

Having now considered the riffraff of the module, we are ready to investigate some
interesting routines.

The function bt_add() adds a new item to a tree following the algorithm described
previously. If a tree is empty the routine calls init_tree() and returns. If a tree is not
empty the application specific comparison routines, passed through at tree initialization
time, are invoked to determine which sub-tree to check next.

Once the next sub-tree is determined, its pointer is stored in addto. This allows later
code to work independent of the sub-tree. The storage of the item occurs next. If the
pointer in the appropriate direction is NULL, we must create a new node and add the item.
If the pointer is not NULL, then we recursively execute this algorithm for the next node in
the appropriate direction.

```
bt_add(newitem)
char *newitem;
{
    struct btnode_type *node, *newnode;
    static struct btnode_type *create_node();
    struct btnode_type **addto; /* Which pointer to extended. */
    static init_tree();

/* If tree is brand new, add to current node.
    --------------------------------------- */
    node = cbt->current_node;
    if (node == NULL) {
        init_tree(newitem);
        return;
    }
/* Determine direction to add to.
    --------------------------- */
    if ((*cbt->less)(newitem, node->item) ||
        (*cbt->eq)   (newitem, node->item)) {
        addto = &(node->left);
    }
    else {
        addto = &(node->right);
    }
```

```
/* If tree in that direction is null, add new node there.
   -------------------------------------------------------- */
   if (*addto == NULL) {
      newnode = create_node();
      moveitem(newitem, newnode->item);
      *addto = newnode;
      bt_setroot();
      return;
   }
/* Otherwise continue search at that subtree.
   --------------------------------------- */
   cbt->current_node = *addto;
   bt_add(newitem);
}
```

The next routine, `traverse()`, traverses the tree, applying the user supplied function `donode()` to each node in the tree. It uses the variables `first` and `second` to store the first and second traversal directions. The logic here is similar to that used with the variable `addto` in the function `bt_add()`. This routine is not callable by client code because it accepts a node. We must try to be strict about keeping such implementation specific details invisible to the client. Clients can call this routine through a front routine called `bt_traverse()`, which is shown immediately following `traverse()`.

```
static traverse(donode, node)
int (*donode) ();
struct btnode_type *node;
{
   struct btnode_type **first, **second;

/* Determine traversal order.
   ------------------------- */
   switch (cbt->trav_direction) {
   case LNR
      first  = &(node->left);
      second = &(node->right);
   break;
   case RNL
      first  = &(node->right);
      second = &(node->left);
   break;
   }
/* Apply donode.
   ------------- */
   if (*first != NULL) traverse(donode, *first);
   (*donode) (node->item);
   if (*second != NULL) traverse(donode, *second);
}
```

```
bt_traverse(donode)
int (*donode) ();
{
    static traverse();
    traverse(donode, cbt->current_node);
}
```

The module is complete. We can now look at a sample application. Consider a program that wants to alphabetize words. First we declare a binary tree and the type of item being stored. In this case the items are character strings.

```
#include "btdef.h"
static struct BINARYTREE wordtree;

struct itemtype {
  char string[40];
};
struct itemtype item;
```

Next, we define the comparison functions. This definition is almost identical to our declaration of the match function in our linked list package example.

```
int less(item1, item2)
struct itemtype *item1, *item2;
{
    if (strcmp(item1->string, item2->string) < 0) return 1;
    else return 0;
}

int eq(item1, item2)
struct itemtype *item1, *item2;
{
    if (!strcmp(item1->string, item2->string)) return 1;
    else return 0;
}
```

We also define the function printit(), which will be recursively applied to each node at tree traversal time.

```
printit(item)
struct itemtype *item;
{
    printf ("%s\n", item->string);
}
```

With this header information in place, we can write our main program, which should be self-explanatory.

```
main()
{
    int less(), eq(), printit();
    bt_settree(&wordtree);
    bt_init(less, eq, LNR, sizeof(struct itemtype));

/* Add words to tree.
   ----------------- */
    bt_add("dog");
    bt_add("cat");
    bt_add("elephant");
    bt_add("gerbil");
    bt_add("ant");
    bt_add("germ");
    bt_add("zebra");
    bt_add("lion");
    bt_add("turtle");
    bt_add("worm");

/* Display words in ascending order.
   -------------------------------- */
    printf ("Ascending order:\n");
    bt_traverse(printit);
}
```

The output from this program looks just like what we hoped for

```
Ascending order:
ant
cat
dog
elephant
gerbil
germ
lion
turtle
worm
zebra
```

11.4. EXERCISES

1. In this chapter we gave pseudocode for an add primitive and traced through the steps in adding a kangaroo. Trace through this algorithm with a few more items, say alligator, gnat, and turtle. Draw the resulting tree.

2. Write two new binary tree primitives, down() and out(), which return the depth and vertical position of the current node relative to the root, respectively. For example, the nodes in the animal tree shown earlier would have these values:

Node	Down	Out
gerbil	0	0
dog	1	-1
rat	1	1
cat	2	-2
zebra	2	2

3. Add code to handle LRN traversal.

4. Write a function bt_settraverse() to reset the direction of traversal for a tree. Modify the test program to print the list once in ascending order, then once in descending order.

5. Add bt_find() which starts searching for an item at the current node. If an item is found, make its node current and return TRUE. If an item is not found, return FALSE, and set the current node to be the node to which the item should be added. Also write bt_retrieve(), which returns the address of the current item.

   Use these functions to write a word counter. This program will analyze a text file and display the words in alphabetical order. It will also display a count of the number of times each word was encountered.

6. Write two more binary tree primitives, left() and right(). These two routines will change the current node's position to the next node on the left or right. Return TRUE if the operation is successful, FALSE if there are no remaining nodes in the requested direction.

7. Write a primitive biggest() which finds the next largest node relative to the current node. The next largest node will then become current. Think carefully about the algorithm you will use. (Hint: the algorithm is recursive.) Also write smallest(), the mirror image of biggest().

8. In Chapter 6, we mentioned the possibility of using a binary tree to speed up cache performance. A linked list cache orders items by relative time of reference. However the list needs to be sequentially scanned to find a particular item. For very large caches, this procedure may prove to be too slow. Construct a binary tree to be used in parallel with the cache. The binary tree elements will point to links in the linked list. When an item is added to the list, a pointer to the link will also be added to the tree. This automatic addition will allow the location of an item within the cache to be quickly located. Rewrite the cache along these lines.

   To correctly construct the binary tree, you will need to delete items from the tree whenever they are removed from the cache, a function we have not yet considered. Your delete() function will probably need the biggest() function from the last problem.

9. Compare the way initialization is handled in the binary tree module and the linked list module. What are the advantages of each technique?

10. Write a routine to free a tree, that is, go through the entire tree and call free() for each piece of memory allocated by malloc().

CHAPTER 12 **Implementation Notes**

The techniques of implementing reusable data structures through package programming are remarkably similar for a wide range of structures. This book has given examples of packages written for linked lists, caches, queues, stacks, and binary trees, a diverse group of structures with quite different functionality goals. In each case however the implementation followed an almost identical pattern. This pattern is important to recognize, because it can form the basis for a wide variety of data manipulation packages, and can provide a method for creating generalized, reusable, and testable code.

A package, as implemented in this book, is made up of two files (and an optional third). These files and their functions, are

- Data Descriptor Header File—this file gives a generic definition of the data structure.
- Executable Code File—this file contains the functions that manipulate the generic data structure.
- Macro Definitions File (Optional)—this file contains macro redefinitions of functions. This file is provided only when necessary for performance reasons.

Let us examine each of these files in more detail.

12.1. DATA DESCRIPTOR HEADER FILE

The goal of the Data Descriptor Header File (DDHF) is to allow a package client to declare one or more instances of a structure without having to be aware of how that structure will be implemented. For example, a linked list package provides a DDHF (lldef.h) to define a linked list. The client then uses this DDHF (via #include <lldef.h>), and declares one or more linked list instances with this statement:

```
struct LINKLIST list1, list2, ...;
```

The program in Chapter 7, a typical example of a linked list client, used the following DDHF to declare two linked list instances.

```
struct LINKLIST curemp, exemp;
```

Remember that one of these lists (curemp) kept track of current employees, and the other (exemp) kept track of ex-employees.

The DDHF for the linked list package looked like this

```
struct LINKTYPE {
  struct LINKTYPE *next;
  struct LINKTYPE *previous;
  char *item;
};

struct LINKLIST {
  struct LINKTYPE *head;
  struct LINKTYPE *tail;
  struct LINKTYPE *clp;

  int listlength;
  int itemlength;

  int (*match) ();
};
```

As you can see, this DDHF neatly packages together all of the elements that define a specific instance of a linked list. These elements include

- A pointer to the head of a list.
- A pointer to the tail of a list.
- A pointer to the "current link" of a list.
- The number of links in the list.
- The size of an item being stored in the list.
- A pointer to a function that compares two items in the list for equality.

All of these linked list elements are variables which are adjusted, and re-adjusted, at run time.

The linked list DDHF also defines a link, the basic building block of the linked list. Links are never seen by the client. They are placed in the DDHF because they are needed in the linked list declaration. For the same reason, we included the definition for binary tree nodes in the binary tree DDHF from Chapter 11.

```
/* btdef.h */

#define LNR 1   /* Left, Node, Right */
#define RNL 2   /* Right, Node, Left */
#define LRN 3   /* Left, Right, Node */

struct btnode_type {
   struct btnode_type *left;
   struct btnode_type *right;
   char *item;
};

struct BINARYTREE {
   struct btnode_type *root;           /* Root of tree.          */
   struct btnode_type *current_node;   /* Current node.          */
   int itemlength;                     /* Size of item in node.  */
   int trav_direction;                 /* Direction of traversal. */
   int (*less)();                      /* Two functions to com-  */
   int (*eq)();                        /* pare items.            */
};
```

Any DDHF contains at least two variables—a pointer to an item (item) and a variable which describes the number of consecutive memory bytes needed to store an item (itemlength).

The item pointer contains the address of client stored data. The primary function of any data manipulation package is to store client items in one or more instances of a data management structure, say a linked list. Even when a client uses only one instance of such a structure, that one instance can potentially contain thousands of items. Each item pointer contains the address of a single item.

The packages in this book assumed item length was invariant for an instance of a structure, thus item length was stored only once per instance. This assumption may not always be valid, in which case each item pointer would need an associated length. There may even be cases in which the length can be inferred, such as when an item is a null terminated string. But, this instance is strictly application specific, and should not be considered as the general case.

A DDHF can vary in complexity. Although the linked list and binary tree DDHFs contain a great deal of information, the queue DDHF, presented in Chapter 9, is essentially nothing more than a redefinition of a queue as a linked list.

```
/* queuedef.h */
#include "lldef.h"

#define qitemsize llsetsize   /* define size of item in queue  */
#define qset llsetlist        /* set current queue             */
#define qlength ll_length     /* Return number of items in queue */

#define QUEUE LINKLIST
```

Another example of a DDHF, one of intermediate complexity, is the cache DDHF. Like the queue DDHF, the cache is built on a linked list. Also like the queue, this foundation is hidden from the client. Unlike the queue, the cache is more than just a linked list under a different guise. The difference is clear from the following cache DDHF:

```
#include "lldef.h"

#define casetmatch llsetmatch
#define caitemsize llsetsize

struct CACHE {
  int cachesize;
  struct LINKLIST clist;
};
```

Although these DDHFs vary in complexity and design, they share a common purpose—to allow the client to declare instances of the structure in question without concern for how that structure will be implemented.

12.2. EXECUTABLE CODE FILE

The second file in your package triad is the Executable Code File (ECF). This file contains header inclusions, a global variable region, and, most important, the function declarations. We will look at each of these areas individually.

12.2.1. ECF—Header Inclusions

The header inclusions consist of one `#include` for each header needed by the ECF. At least one header is always needed, the DDHF for the package. For example, from the linked list ECF (Chapter 5)

```
#include <lldef.h>
```

And, from the cache ECF (Chapter 8)

```
#include <cadef.h>
```

Sequestering the structure definition into the DDHF assures that the structure definition as seen by the client code and by the ECF is always in sync, or at least can be put back into sync by a simple recompile.

12.2.2. ECF—Global Variable Region

The global variable region of the ECF is a sparse collection of static variables. The one variable you can count on finding (at least in our implementations) is the Current Structure

Pointer (CSP). We have gone to considerable effort to allow multiple structure instances to be manipulated. In fact Chapter 5 is devoted to this topic. Although several methods for resolving structure currency were considered, the one we settled on was maintaining a CSP in each packet. The CSP for the linked list packet, `list`, tells us which specific linked list is manipulated when a linked list operator is invoked.

The definition of a CSP always follows this general pattern:

```
static struct structname *CSPname;
```

For example, from the linked list ECF (Chapter 5)

```
static struct LINKLIST *list;
```

And, from the cache ECF (Chapter 8)

```
static struct CACHE *ca;
```

And, from the queue ECF (Chapter 9)

```
static struct QUEUE *q;
```

And finally, from the binary tree ECF (Chapter 11)

```
static struct BINARYTREE *cbt;
```

The CSP is the only global variable found in our ECFs. The reason so few global variables are used in our implementations is that most of the global variables one might expect have already been accounted for in the DDHF. In fact, the procedure for supporting multiple structure instances, as described in Chapter 5, is largely a process of moving variables from the global variable region into the DDHF.

Other global variables could certainly be used. If, for example, one wanted to keep track of the total number of linked lists initialized, an easy method would be to keep a count in a static variable declared in this region.

The CSP, as well as other global variables we have alluded to, have all been declared `static`, to prevent them from being accidentally modified by user code. In some cases, you may want to give up some of this protection for other considerations. In Chapter 6 we showed how macro definitions could be used to speed up performance, but only if most of the global variables, in particular the CSP, were allowed to be externally referenced.

12.2.3. ECF—Function Definitions

The rest of the ECF is occupied by function definitions and their close cousins, macro definitions. In general, functions fall into one of three groups:

- **Initializers**—functions that clients use to initialize one or more aspects of their generic data structures.

- **Operators**—functions that clients use to manipulate their structures.
- **Internal Functions**—functions used by other functions in the package. Macro definitions can be thought of as a category of internal functions.

12.2.3.1. Initializer functions
There are many initializer functions, but one in particular is always present—the Current Structure Pointer Reset (CSPR). This function sets the CSP to a particular structure instance provided by the client. This function follows this general pattern:

```
CSPR_name (local_structure_pointer)
struct STRUCTURE_TYPE *local_structure_pointer;
{
  CSP = local_structure_pointer;
  other initializing events;
}
```

For example, the following CSPR comes from the linked list ECF (Chapter 5)

```
llsetlist(new_list)
struct LINKLIST *new_list;
{
  list = new_list;
}
```

From the cache ECF (Chapter 8) comes the following CSPR:

```
casetcache(newcache)
struct CACHE *newcache;
{
  ca = newcache;
  llsetlist (&ca->clist);
}
```

The CSPR `casetcache()` invokes another CSPR, `llsetlist()`, which is from the linked list package. The cache is built on top of the linked list, and the cache operators are built on top of linked list operators. This CSPR not only sets up the current cache, but also sets up the linked list package to work on the cache linked list. If the cache implementation would change (see, for example, Exercise 11.8) the call to `llsetlist()` would probably be eliminated, or at least modified. This change should be transparent to the cache client, because the existence and calling sequence of `casetcache()` would most likely be unaffected.

The CSPR may sometimes exist in spirit rather than substance. For instance, the queue ECF (Chapter 9) does not contain a CSPR. The CSPR was omitted because the queue was redefined in its DDHF as a linked list. Thus many of the queue operators were redefined linked list operators, including the CSPR. This particular redefinition occurred in the following line of the DDHF:

```
#define qset llsetlist
```

This same process was used for stacks (Chapter 10).

The purposes of the remaining initializer functions tend to be structure specific. In general, they make up a collection of run time gates used by the client to define or redefine various aspects of the structure. From the linked list ECF we have these examples of initializers:

```
llsetmatch(numatch) /* Initializes the match function. */
int (*numatch) ();
{
  list->match = numatch;
}


llsetsize(size) /* Set the storage requirements for the list. */
int size;
{
  list->itemlength = size;
}


llinit(newitem) /* Initialize the structure. */
char *newitem;
{
  struct LINKTYPE *llcrlink();

  list->head = list->tail = list->clp = llcrlink();
  list->clp->next = list->clp->previous = NULL;
  moveitem(newitem, list->clp->item);
  list->listlength  = 1;
}
```

There is no reason why one initializer function can not serve double, triple, or even greater duty, as in the following from the binary tree ECF (Chapter 11)

```
bt_init(btless,bteq, btdirect, btsize)
int (*btless)();    /* Function to see if item 1 less than item 2. */
int (*bteq)();      /* Function to see if item 1 equal to item 2.  */
int btdirect;       /* Set the traversal direction. */
int btsize;         /* Size of an item in this tree. */
{
  cbt->root = NULL;
  cbt->current_node = NULL;
  cbt->less = btless;
  cbt->eq = bteq;
  cbt->trav_direction = btdirect;
  cbt->itemlength = btsize;
}
```

When combining initializing functions like this example, you need to consider the best interests of your clients and consider how they will feel about resetting all of these elements when any one of them need to be changed.

12.2.3.2. Operator functions
From your clients' perspectives, the operator functions are the most critical. These functions map on a more or less one to one basis to the operations clients expect to perform on a given structure. A typical example is st_push(), from the stack packet, which maps to the stack *push* function. Another is llnext(), from the linked list packet, which maps to the *next link* function.

Most of the functionality of an operator function is defined by the individual operation, however there is usually some design flexibility. In particular, the person responsible for implementation decides how to handle the odd conditions, such as termination. For example, a decision must be made concerning what the next link function should do upon encountering an end of list. Should we leave the Current Link Pointer unchanged and return FALSE or reset the list to the beginning and return TRUE? Careful consideration needs to be given as to how these functions will be used. Such functions are often embedded in constructs such as for() loops, and termination behavior will have ramifications on how gracefully clients can exit the loop.

The function llnext() from Chapter 5 assumed that upon reaching the end of a list, clients would want nothing done, but would like a return code indicating that the end of the list was reached. The following segment from the cache package (Chapter 8) is typical of this routine's use.

```
ca_check(lookfor) /* See if item is in cache */
                  /* Return TRUE or FALSE     */
struct itemtype *lookfor;
{
    struct itemtype lookat;
    cmpitem();

    llhead();
    for (;;) {
        llretrieve (&lookat);
        if (cmpitem(lookfor, &lookat)) {
            lldelete();
            lladdhead(&lookat);
            return (1);
        }
        if (lllnext())
            return (0);
    }
}
```

12.2.3.3. Internal functions
The last of the functions are the internal functions. From your clients' perspectives, these are the least important because they are invisible.

From your perspective, these functions make your code better modularized and therefore your life a little easier.

A good example of such a function is `llcrlink()`, from Chapter 5. This routine takes care of the dirty details of allocating both a new link and the space for its associated item. Because this functionality is needed in several procedures, a separate function is created. And because clients do not use this functionality, it is declared static.

```
static struct LINKTYPE *llcrlink()
{
  char *malloc();
  struct LINKTYPE *link;
  link = (struct LINKTYPE *) malloc(sizeof(struct
        LINKTYPE));
  link->item= malloc(list->itemlength);
  return(link);
}
```

12.3. MACRO DEFINITIONS FILE

The Macro Definitions File (MDF) is optional. It is used in cases where performance is absolutely critical, and the overhead of the function calls for data structure manipulation cannot be tolerated. This book gives only one example of an MDF. It can be found in Chapter 6 for the linked list packet. As discussed in that chapter, performance is generally a poorly understood issue. You are discouraged from jumping into an MDF unless you absolutely must for performance reasons. You will pay for any improvements in performance with increased debugging difficulty, decreased code readability, and loss of control. In most cases there are better ways to increase performance than by adding an MDF.

12.4. SUMMARY

The overall structure of a data manipulation package, as presented in this chapter, can be easily illustrated. The following diagram shows all of the various components of the package.

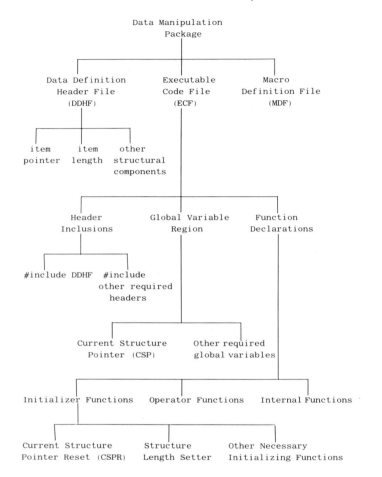

12.5. EXERCISES

1. Add a function to the linked list package called llcount(), which returns the number of initialized linked lists.

2. Categorize each function in the binary tree package as either Initializer, Operator, or Internal Function. If a function does not fit neatly into one of these three categories, explain why.

3. Choose a data structure not represented in this book. Define the necessary operators. Create a reusable data manipulation package for the structure. Describe how each of the components described in this chapter are implemented in your package.

4. When discussing the DDHF, we pointed out that its implementation assumes an invariant itemlength for a given structure instance. Show the modifications that are required to a package if this invariance is not so. Use the linked list package for your analysis.

CHAPTER 13 **Package Design Rules**

13.1. OVERVIEW

Chapter 12 summarized the development of reusable packages with a formal, perhaps even pedantic, design overview. This chapter takes a slightly less constrained approach, summarizing the information presented in this book with five rules of well organized package design. They are

- Rule 1. Identify Your Data Structures.
- Rule 2. Generalize Your Data Structures.
- Rule 3. Make Your Code Inspectable.
- Rule 4. Separate Natural Antagonists From Each Other.
- Rule 5. Keep Performance in Perspective.

Actually these rules, or at least variants on them, would serve you well in any software development endeavor. Let us look at each of them in detail.

13.2. THE RULES

RULE 1. IDENTIFY YOUR DATA STRUCTURES

Identifying the data structures indigenous to a programming problem may or may not be a trivial task. Chapter 11 contained a program that alphabetized words, a problem that immediately suggested the use of a some kind of tree structure. On the other hand, Chapter 3 described this problem:

> Consider writing a program to scan text files looking for overused words. Let's say a word is overused if it appears more than once within any given stretch of 25 unique words.

The data structures needed to solve this problem were not at all obvious; many programmers might not even have recognized the basic mechanisms of a cache at play here.

Most programs probably fall in between these two extreme examples. A good example of this first rule is the Memory Allocator of Chapter 10, described like this

> By now you should be familiar with the standard C functions `malloc()` and `free()`. We will now write similar, but easier to use functions. A program is expected to call `free()` once for every call made to `malloc()`. This call fulfills its responsibility to return memory to the dynamic memory pool once the memory is no longer needed. We will write three functions with these characteristics:
>
> - `get_mem()`—This procedure works exactly like `malloc()`. It accepts one parameter, the number of memory bytes needed, and returns a pointer to a memory block.
> - `mark_stack()`—This procedure, with no parameters, marks a moment in time.
> - `rel_mem()`—This procedure releases all memory allocated with `get_mem()` since the last call to `mark_stack()`.
>
> These three functions allow a user to mark a moment of time in the stack, allocate several chunks of memory, and then, with one call to `rel_mem()`, release all memory chunks allocated since the time was marked.

Although the data structure requirements are not completely obvious here, the passage contains some suggestive clues. This problem is describing what is essentially a roll-back in time, or a return to a previous state. The previous state is the moment when `mark_stack()` was last called. Temporal roll-backs, or suggestions of a look back to a previous state, are often associated with stacks. Indeed, the stack was the data structure used to solve this problem.

Other data structures have other identifying behaviors. A program that needs to allow events to occur in the same order as they were initiated will probably use a queue. A program that works with a small subset of a larger universe will use a cache. A program that wants to access items by a unique key will probably use either some type of tree, or some type of hash structure.

Identifying a data structure means more than just being able to name it. You should be able to give a full conceptual description of the data structure, including expectations of its behavior. You also must give an accounting of the structure's operators, or primitives. For example, a linked list was described in Chapter 3 as being analogous to a train, and searching for an item in a list like searching for an item on a train. This description was conceptual of the data structure. The operators if you recall, included these

llnext()	Move to the next link.
llprevious()	Move to the previous link.
llretrieve()	Retrieve the item in the current link.
lladd()	Create a new link with this item immediately after the current link.
lldelete()	Delete the current link. Join the previous and next links together.

Any analysis of a programming problem must include an analysis of the underlying data structures. Analyzing these data structures, which represent and manipulate your program's information, is every bit as important as analyzing any of the other algorithms that make up your program. Such an analysis must include a complete description of each data structure including its behavior, operators, and expectations.

RULE 2. GENERALIZE YOUR DATA STRUCTURES

Generalizing your data structures affords you several advantages. Your code will be more reusable. If you do not appreciate this advantage today, you will tomorrow. Your code will also be more testable and therefore more reliable, an advantage you *will* enjoy immediately.

The process of generalization is a two-stage process. First you must determine which aspects of the data structure are application specific. Second, you must make those aspects definable at run time (or at compile time, if you want to take a wishy-washy approach).

The application specifics are not always obvious, and some will probably be debatable. For example, in the linked list first described in Chapter 3, the description of the item being stored in the list was certainly application specific. But it was not obvious then that searching for the item would involve an application specific match function. This issue did not arise until Chapter 5.

Other linked list features could have been debatably nominated for application specificity. Two-way versus one-way lists was one such issue considered in Exercise 7-2. The maximum size of the list in the exercise could have been application specific. The manner of dealing with error conditions could certainly have been application specific, and managed much like the application specific matching function.

The point is not that you should generalize to the absolute n^{th} degree. This type of generalization is almost impossible, and probably not even desirable. Rather you should be aware of what aspects of code tend to be application specific, and strive to make your code as general as is reasonable. Also, the areas in which you have chosen not to generalize, be aware of the tradeoffs you have made, and the limitations you have accepted.

RULE 3. MAKE YOUR CODE INSPECTABLE

Write code so that it can be subjected to an inspection process, and the proper workings of your functions verified. The relationship between inspectability and variable complexity was examined in Chapter 2. The inspectability of a piece of code was shown to be inversely proportional to the product of the number of variables involved and the number of states those variables could accept. In other words, code became more complex as it used more variables, and as those variables took on a larger number of significant values. We can formulate the following as a hypothetical measure of code complexity

```
CC = NV * NS
  CC = Code Complexity
  NV = Number of variables
  NS = Number of states
```

As you observe functions with increasing NV and NS values, it is easy to believe that their overall complexities are increasing as well. Consider this routine from Chapter 5, which set the current link in a linked list to the head of a list

```
llhead()
{
  list->clp = list->head;
}
```

Ignoring error conditions, llhead() has

```
CC = NV * NS = 2 * 1 = 2
```

The routine is very believable, almost trivial, and requires little time for an exhaustive inspection.

From Chapter 8 comes the routine ca_add(), which added a new item to a cache

```
ca_add(newitem) /* Add a new item to the cache */
struct itemtype *newitem;
{
/* Add item to list.
   ---------------- */
   if (ll_length() == 0)
      llinit(newitem);
   else
      lladdhead(newitem);

/* Delete an old item if cache is overloaded.
   ---------------------------------------- */
   if (ll_length() > cachesize) {
      lltail();
      lldelete();
   }
}
```

This routine has three variables, newitem, cachesize and ll_length; and three significant states:

```
State 1: ll_length == 0 && ll_length <  cachesize
State 2: ll_length > 0  && ll_length <  cachesize
State 3: ll_length > 0  && ll_length == cachesize
```

This configuration gives ca_add() a CC rating of 9, or a rating 4 1/2 times as complicated as llhead().

Next consider the routine bt_add() from Chapter 11, which added an item to a binary tree

```
bt_add(newitem)
char *newitem;
{
    struct btnode_type *node, *newnode;
    static struct btnode_type *create_node();
    struct btnode_type **addto; /* Which pointer to extended. */
    static init_tree();

/* If tree is brand new, add to current node.
   ---------------------------------------- */
    node = cbt->current_node;
    if (node == NULL) {
        init_tree(newitem);
        return;
    }
/* Determine direction to add to.
   --------------------------- */
    if ((*cbt->less)(newitem, node->item) ||
        (*cbt->eq)   (newitem, node->item)) {
        addto = &(node->left);
    }
    else {
        addto = &(node->right);
    }
/* If tree in that direction is null, add new node there.
   --------------------------------------------------- */
    if (*addto == NULL) {
        newnode = create_node();
        moveitem(newitem, newnode->item);
        *addto = newnode;
        bt_setroot();
        return;
    }
/* Otherwise continue search at that subtree.
   --------------------------------------- */
    cbt->current_node = *addto;
    bt_add(newitem);
}
```

This routine has three static variables, one parameter, and three members of the global structure cbt in use, giving us a total NV value of 7. We can list at least these five states:

```
State 1:  cbt = NULL
State 2:  cbt != NULL
State 3:  newitem < cbt->current_node->item
State 4:  newitem == cbt->current_node->item
State 5:  newitem > cbt->current_node->item
```

The CC value for `bt_add()` is around 7 * 5, or 35.

Is it true that `llhead()`, with a CC rating of 2, is about 1/5 as complex as `ca_add()`, rated at 9? Or that `bt_add()`, with a CC rating of 35, is almost 4 times as complex as `ca_add()`? It is hard to know how closely these numbers correspond to reality, although they seem within reason. `llhead()`, rated at 2, certainly seems simple enough. `ca_add()`, rated at 9, seems more complicated, but still manageable. `bt_add()`, rated at 35, seems, at least to the author, to be at the very limits of manageability.

Another relevant concept of this rule is that of the "inspectable unit", or a unit of code inspected as a whole. We have assumed inspectable units to be nothing short of whole functions. The routine `bt_add()`, one might argue, should really be considered two inspectable units—one that deals with the case of `cbt` equal to NULL, and the other with the case of `cbt` not equal to NULL. This consideration may indeed be true, but one message is still clear. Your code will be easier to understand, and more inspectable, if you minimize both the number of variables your code uses, and the number of variable states that affect your code.

RULE 4. SEPARATE NATURAL ANTAGONISTS FROM EACH OTHER

Rule 4 can be restated as two sub-rules.

- Protect your clients from your code.
- Protect your code from your clients.

Clients are protected from your code when they can use your packages without having to be aware of implementation. The client is, of course, responsible for abiding by the rules of your packages. For example, a client of the queue (Chapter 9) has these responsibilities

- At the beginning of their module
  `#include "queuedef.h"`
- Declare the queue with a statement like
  `static struct QUEUE queue_name`
  where `queue_name` is a variable name of the client's choice.
- Anytime the current queue changes, the client must reset it with the routine `qset()`.
  `qset(queue_name)`
- Etc.

Your clients must be protected from changes in package implementation. Although the queue package was implemented as a linked list, the client interface was insulated from any possible changes in the implementation. The queue could easily have changed to an array implementation with little, if any, effect on the client, other than a possible recompilation if the DDHF was modified. A good example of the care we took in adhering to this rule is in the DDHF `queuedef.h`:

```
#include "lldef.h"

#define quitemsize llsetsize    /* define size of item in queue  */
#define qset llsetlist          /* set current queue             */
#define qlength ll_length       /* Return number of items in queue */

#define QUEUE LINKLIST
```

This header file redefines queue terminology as linked list terminology. Clients could have been told to use, for example, the procedure `llsetsize()` rather than `qitemsize()`, but then they would have been required to make radical code changes if we had ever abandoned the linked list implementation. The use of this header file protects our clients from idiosyncratic implementations.

We cannot promise to totally insulate clients from future modifications. We can promise to take every effort to minimize such modifications however. For example, Chapter 3 developed a cache package based on a linked list package. This linked list package was extensively modified in Chapters 4 and 5, and the cache package was upgraded in Chapter 8. The result of these changes was the developoment of linked list and cache packages that were largely run-time definable.

Because of these changes, Chapter 3 cache package clients had to add some new code to declare, at runtime, both the name of the current cache and the nature of items being stored. In return for this addition, they were able to have multiple caches available, each storing different types of items. Obviously we were not completely successful in protecting our clients from later changes; however, considering the extensive nature of the changes we made, the effect on clients was quite small.

The second part of Rule 4 stated that you must protect your code from your clients. Keep any global variables static and limit client access to specific, well defined gates. From Chapter 8 comes this cache function which sets the maximum cache size:

```
casetsize(size)
int size;
{
  ca->cachesize = size;
}
```

No functional reason exists for providing `casetsize()`. Clients can set `cache_name.cachesize` to the requested cache size almost as easily with an arithmetic assignment as through a function call. Programmers concerned with performance might even make the misguided argument that eliminating the function saves the overhead of a function call.

The function `casetsize()` serves two purposes. It protects our clients from any possible changes in the cache structure. And it limits client access to a single, well defined gate. We even have the opportunity to do some sanity checks on the size of the cache. For example, we can add code to catch non-positive integers, or positive integers whose value is suspect.

You can also use function calls to provide access to global variables on a read-only, need-to-know basis. For example, the following linked list function gives read-only access to the length of the current list

```
ll_length()
{
  return (list->listlength);
}
```

Similar read-only functions for a binary tree are requested as part of Exercise 11-2. The reader was to write the functions down() and out(), describing the relationship between the current node and the root node. The obvious solution calls for two new variables to be added to the binary tree structure, some code changes to existing functions to maintain these variables, and the creation of down() and out() to provide read-only access.

As desirable as it may be to completely sequester clients from our variables, we have shown a willingness to compromise in this area. We have done so to support the principal of generalization, and also, when necessary, for run-time performance.

We can see the sacrifices made for generalization by looking at the linked list structure as it existed in Chapter 3. Back then our package allowed only a single linked list and the item definition of its contents was determined once and for all at compile time. With no possible question about which particular linked list we were working with, the linked list structure was defined, allocated, and completely sequestered inside the module.

By the end of Chapter 5, the linked list package had changed quite a bit. Clients could create thousands of linked lists, as many as they needed. Along with this increased flexibility came increased responsibility. Clients were now required to allocate memory for these lists, and to let the package know which list to use at any one time. Because of these new responsibilities, clients could not be prevented from modifying basic linked list structural components (after all, they *did* pay for the memory). All in all, the improvements in package functionality made this danger worthwhile.

We further compromised in Chapter 6 for the sake of performance. To replace function calls by macro definitions, we changed what had been a static declaration of list, the variable that told us which linked list was current, to a global declaration. This change allowed the macro expansions to directly manipulate the current list. Unfortunately, there is no way to limit manipulation of this variable to macros, and clients can intentionally or unintentionally corrupt this variable. If corruption happens, our package code ceases to work. This compromise hurts more than the first, and seems to buy us less benefit, but it does demonstrate that we are not totally inflexible.

RULE 5. KEEP PERFORMANCE IN PERSPECTIVE

Performance problems are usually caused by a poor choice in data structures, algorithms, or both. They are not usually caused by over-modularization or over-generalization. The temptation to ignore the principals of modularization and generalization in hopes of increased performance is omnipresent and, in many cases, omnipotent in this business. These hopes are usually false.

Of course modularization does not *ipso facto* guarantee intelligent design. You will occasionally run into code which, although highly modularized, is so poorly organized that performance has taken a beating, such as the following code segment

```c
#include <stdio.h>
main()
{
  FILE *input, *prep();
  int n, offset;
  char string[10000];

/* Read a 10,000 byte string.
   ------------------------- */
  for (n=0; n<10000; n+=100) {
    input = prep("data", "rb");
    readit (&string[n], n, input);
  }
}
FILE *prep(str1, str2)
char *str1, *str2;
{
  FILE *fopen(), *unit;

/* Open requested file, if error quit.
   ---------------------------------- */
  if ((unit = fopen(str1, str2)) == NULL) {
    printf ("Bad file open\n");
    exit(0);
  }
/* If no error, return file unit.
   ---------------------------- */
  return (unit);
}
```

```
readit (string, n, input)
char *string;
int n;
FILE *input;
{
/* Set file pointer to requested string.
   ------------------------------------ */
    fseek (input, n, 0);

/* Read string and null terminate.
   ----------------------------- */
    fread (string, 100, 1, input);
    string[100] = '\0';

/* Close file and return.
   --------------------- */
    fclose (input);
}
```

Obviously this code needs rewrite help.

Performance problems more often resemble the bottleneck described for word caches in Chapter 6, where we saw a very slow cache mechanism for large cache sizes. At first glance, modularization appeared to be causing a major loss of performance, with 65% of our runtime devoted to package overhead. However on closer examination, the dominant performance problem turned out to be not in the *modularization* of the linked list, but in the decision to *use* a linked list in the first place.

In fact, the cache's package design can actually aid our ability to work with performance. The cache user should be completely shielded from the algorithmic details of a cache. Once a cache package is isolated as the performance gate, it can be redesigned with little, if any, impact on the user (see Exercise 11-8).

Finally, as we already pointed out, C the programming language offers good tools for reconciling performance with modularization. In Chapter 6 we discussed using specific C tools, macro definitions, to improve performance while minimizing the loss of logical modularization.

13.3. SUMMARY

This book has introduced several fundamental data structures. By now you should understand linked lists, caches, queues, priority queues, stacks, and binary trees. You should have a reasonable introduction also to recursive structures. You should have an excellent understanding of the package approach to data structure implementation, and be able to extend this understanding to new structures.

This book is just the beginning. We have not even touched upon many common structures such as sets, graphs, relations, B-trees and tries. Other important structures have been introduced only informally, such as the hash cache (Exercise 9-4), the cache tree (Exercise 10-11), and disk oriented structures (Exercise 11-11). If you are not yet familiar with these concepts, attend a formal course in Data Structures.

Our general understanding of data structures is continuing to evolve. The field of information management, for one, is constantly pushing and expanding the limits of data structures. There is great incentive to store more information in less space with faster access times. Current journals in Computer Science contain many examples of new data structures being developed to address this need. Keep abreast of new developments.

Good programmers have a good understanding of data structures. They understand how to use and implement different structures. They can choose appropriate structures for a particular problem and fully understand implementation tradeoffs. Data structures are the primary trade tools of software engineering. As a software engineer, it is your responsibility to know what these tools do, how to use them, and when new and better ones become available.

Index

C/UNIX Order Form

Prentice Hall Publishers will continue to make available the First Edition of <u>The C Programming Language</u> by Kernighan and Ritchie for programmers using compilers developed prior to the Draft Proposed ANSI Standard. To order copies of this title as well as the other books in our C/UNIX list, kindly complete this form.

QUANTITY	TITLE/AUTHOR (abbreviated)	ISBN	PRICE	TOTAL
_____	The C Programming Language, 1/E, Kernighan/Ritchie	013-110163-3	$29.00 paper	_____
_____	The C Programming Language, 2/E, Kernighan/Ritchie	013-110362-8	$30.00 paper	_____
		013-110370-9	$42.00 cloth	_____
_____	The C Answer Book, 1/E, Tondo/Gimpel	013-109877-2	$22.00 paper	_____
_____	The C Answer Book, 2/E, Tondo/Gimpel	013-109653-2	$21.33 paper	_____
_____	ANSI C: A Lexical Guide, The Mark Williams Company	013-037814-3	$38.00 paper	_____
_____	UNIX Sys V Programmer's Guide, AT&T	013-940438-4	$34.95 paper	_____
_____	UNIX Sys V STREAMS Primer, AT&T	013-940529-1	$21.95 paper	_____
_____	UNIX Sys V STREAMS Prog's Guide, AT&T	013-940537-2	$24.95 paper	_____
_____	UNIX Sys V Network Prog's Guide, AT&T	013-940461-9	$24.95 paper	_____
_____	UNIX Sys V Prog's Ref Man, AT&T	013-940479-1	$34.95 paper	_____
_____	UNIX Sys V User's Ref Man, AT&T	013-940487-2	$34.95 paper	_____
_____	UNIX Sys V User's Guide, 2/E, AT&T	013-940545-3	$24.95 paper	_____
_____	UNIX Sys V Utilities Release Notes, AT&T	013-940552-6	$21.95 paper	_____
_____	AT&T Computer Software Catalog: UNIX System V Software	013-050154-9	$23.95 paper	_____
_____	AT&T Computer Software Catalog: Workstation Software	013-050162-X	$22.95 paper	_____
_____	UNIX Sys User's Handbook, Bolsky	013-937764-6	$18.95 paper	_____
_____	UNIX For People, Birns, et al.	013-937442-6	$30.95 paper	_____
_____	UNIX Primer, Lomuto, et al.	013-937731-X	$28.95 paper	_____
_____	UNIX Ref Guide, McNulty	013-938957-0	$28.95 paper	_____
_____	DOS: UNIX Systems, Seyer/Mills	013-218645-4	$29.95 paper	_____
_____	Design of UNIX O/S, Bach	013-201799-7	$44.00 paper	_____
_____	Operating System Des: XINU Approach, Comer	013-637539-1	$50.00 cloth	_____
_____	Oper Sys. Design: Internetworking, Comer	013-637414-X	$50.00 cloth	_____
_____	Oper Sys Des & Implementation, Tanenbaum	013-637406-9	$46.00 cloth	_____
	MINIX for the IBM PC/XT/AT:			
	1) 512K for the AT	013-584418-5	$116.00	_____
	2) 640K for the PC/ PC XT	013-584426-6	$116.00	_____
	3) MINIX for the IBM PC/XT/AT Reference Manual	013-584400-2	$28.00 paper	_____
_____	UNIX Prog Environment, Kernighan/Pike	013-937681-X	$24.95 paper	_____
_____	Advanced UNIX Prog, Rochkind	013-011800-1	$34.95 paper	_____
_____	Portable C & UNIX Sys Prog, Lapin	013-686494-5	$29.95 paper	_____
_____	MIP: R2000 RISC Architecture, Kane	013-584749-4	$24.95 paper	_____
_____	UNIX Relational Database Management, Manis	013-938622-X	$37.00 paper	_____
_____	UNIX Sys Software Readings	013-938358-1	$21.95 paper	_____
_____	UNIX Sys Readings & Applications, I, AT&T	013-938532-0	$21.00 paper	_____
_____	UNIX Sys Readings & Applications, II, AT&T	013-939845-7	$21.00 paper	_____
_____	vi User's Handbook, Bolsky	013-941733-8	$18.95 paper	_____
_____	Guide to vi, Sonnenschein	013-371311-3	$21.95 paper	_____
_____	Troff Typesetting, Emerson, et al.	013-930959-4	$27.95 paper	_____

(over, please)

QUANTITY	TITLE/AUTHOR (abbreviated)	ISBN	PRICE	TOTAL
_____	Intro to Compiler Construction, Schreiner, et al.	013-474396-2	$41.00 cloth	_____
_____	UNIX C Shell Field Gde., Anderson, et al.	013-937468-X	$28.95 paper	_____
_____	Preparing Documents w. UNIX, Brown, et al.	013-699976-X	$28.95 cloth	_____
_____	C Answer Book, Tondo, et al.	013-109877-2	$22.00 paper	_____
_____	Advanced C Programming, Rochkind	013-010240-7	$34.95 paper	_____
_____	C Trainer, Feuer	013-109745-8	$27.00 paper	_____
_____	C: A Reference Manual, 2/E, Harbison, et al.	013-109802-0	$27.00 paper	_____
_____	C Companion, Holub	013-109786-5	$24.00 paper	_____
_____	Programming in C w/Bit of UNIX, Moore	013-730094-8	$26.95 paper	_____
_____	Learning To Program in C, Plum	013-527847-3	$35.00 paper	_____
_____	C Notes, Zahn	013-109778-4	$21.95 paper	_____
_____	C Prog in Berkeley UNIX Envirmnt, Horspool	013-109977-9	$31.00 paper	_____
_____	C Programmer's Hndbk, Bolsky	013-110073-4	$23.95 paper	_____
_____	Crafting C Tools, Campbell	013-188418-2	$26.95 paper	_____
_____	C Puzzle Book, Feuer	013-109926-4	$26.00 cloth	_____
_____	Numerical Sftware Tools in C, Kempf	013-627274-6	$34.00 paper	_____
_____	C Programming Guidelines, Plum	013-109992-2	$37.00 paper	_____
_____	A Software Tools Sampler, Miller	013-822305-X	$28.00 paper	_____
_____	Systems Software Tools, Biggerstaff	013-881764-2	$19.95 paper	_____
_____	Clipper 32-Bit Microproc. Manual, Fairchild	013-138058-3	$25.00 paper	_____
		TOTAL		_____

SAVE!

If payment accompanies order, plus your state's sales tax where applicable, Prentice Hall pays postage and handling charges. Same return privilege refund guaranteed. Please do not mail in cash.

☐ **PAYMENT ENCLOSED**—shipping and handling to be paid by publisher (please include your state's tax where applicable).

☐ **SEND BOOKS ON 15-DAY TRIAL BASIS** & bill me (with small charge for shipping and handling).

Name _____

Address _____

City _____ State _____ Zip _____

I prefer to charge my ☐ Visa   ☐ MasterCard

Card Number _____ Expiration Date _____

Signature _____

All prices listed are subject to change without notice.
OFFER NOT VALID OUTSIDE U.S.

MAIL YOUR ORDER TO: Prentice Hall, Book Distribution Center, Route 59 at
Brook Hill Drive, West Nyack, NY 10994

Attention Corporate Customers: For orders over 20 copies to be billed to a corporate address, call (201) 592-2498.

For individuals ordering fewer than 20 copies, call (201) 767-5937.

Prentice Hall C/UNIX Titles Are Available At Better Bookstores